ORGAN STOPS
AND THEIR USE

ORGAN STOPS
AND THEIR USE

BY

REGINALD WHITWORTH, M.B.E.

Author of "The Electric Organ," "A Student's
Guide to the Organ," etc.

LONDON
SIR ISAAC PITMAN & SONS, LTD.

First published 1951
Reprinted 1956

SIR ISAAC PITMAN & SONS, Ltd.
PITMAN HOUSE, PARKER STREET, KINGSWAY, LONDON, W.C.2
THE PITMAN PRESS, BATH
PITMAN HOUSE, BOUVERIE STREET, CARLTON, MELBOURNE
27 BECKETTS BUILDINGS, PRESIDENT STREET, JOHANNESBURG

ASSOCIATED COMPANIES

PITMAN MEDICAL PUBLISHING COMPANY, Ltd.
45 NEW OXFORD STREET, LONDON, W.C.I

PITMAN PUBLISHING CORPORATION
2 WEST 45TH STREET, NEW YORK

SIR ISAAC PITMAN & SONS (CANADA), Ltd.
(INCORPORATING THE COMMERCIAL TEXT BOOK COMPANY)
PITMAN HOUSE, 381–383 CHURCH STREET, TORONTO

MADE IN GREAT BRITAIN AT THE PITMAN PRESS, BATH
E6—(G.392)

PREFACE

THE main purpose of this book is to lead the player to a wider appreciation of the possibilities of organ registration, and to exploit these to the fullest artistic extent. I have found that many organists are handicapped by a lack of knowledge as to how their instrument actually functions.

Part I therefore deals with this aspect with more particular reference to the stops themselves. In order that the subject may be grasped more readily I have made several simplified diagrams, in which technical details have been reduced to a minimum, and in which the working parts have been proportionally exaggerated.

Part II deals with the actual *use* of the stops.

About 1936, or a little earlier, I drafted some fairly comprehensive "Notes on Registration." Soon after this, however, I became involved in preparing the second edition of my book *The Electric Organ*, and the notes were laid aside and forgotten. They remained so until I received from my esteemed and valued friend, the late Lt.-Col. George Dixon, T.D., M.A., a draft of an article he was writing on "Registration from the Listener's Point of View," since published in the quarterly *The Organ*. I was at once struck by the remarkable similarity of many of his ideas with those expressed in my own "Notes," written some years before I had the great privilege of his personal friendship. I therefore looked them up and sent them to him. On his advice I made the notes the basis of the present book, and added much new matter. I wish to express my deep gratitude to him for many suggestions, and for much practical help in its compilation.

I wish also to express my sincere thanks to George T. Thalben-Ball, D.Mus., F.R.C.O., for his great kindness in accepting the dedication of this book, which was in no small measure inspired by his fine and erudite playing, and to Frank W. Haywood, F.R.C.O. (CHM.), L.R.A.M., for kindly reading the proofs.

R. W.

CONTENTS

Preface . . . . PAGE vii

PART ONE: ORGAN STOPS

CHAP.
I. THE ACTION OF THE STOP 3
II. THE STOP KEY 16
III. THE STOPS TO BE FOUND IN BRITISH ORGANS . 21

PART TWO: THE USE OF ORGAN STOPS

IV. DIAPASONS, FULL ORGAN, AND TUBAS . . 33
V. STRING TONE 40
VI. IMITATIVE REEDS 43
VII. FLUTE TONE 44
VIII. MUTATION STOPS 47
IX. MIXTURES (COMPOUND STOPS) . . . 51
X. PEDAL STOPS 54
XI. COUPLERS 59
XII. THE TREMULANT 66
XIII. THE VOX HUMANA 67
XIV. DEVICES TO AID REGISTRATION . . . 69
XV. DOUBLE TOUCH 80
XVI. SUSTAINERS 87
XVII. ORGAN PERCUSSIONS 90
XVIII. CONTINENTAL STOP CONTROL AND REGISTRATION
I—FRENCH 93
XIX. CONTINENTAL STOP CONTROL AND REGISTRATION
II—GERMANY AND OTHER COUNTRIES . . 101
XX. THE BAROQUE REVIVAL 108
XXI. IN CONCLUSION 113
Index 115

ix

ILLUSTRATIONS

The Largest Organ in the World, in the Municipal
Auditorium, Atlantic City, U.S.A.. . *Frontispiece*

PLATE   FACING PAGE

I. England's Largest Organ: Modern "Willis" Console, 38
Liverpool Cathedral . . . . . .

II. Compton Console (Luminous Stop Touches), Southampton Guildhall 39

III. Walker Console, Doncaster Parish Church, Built to the
Design of the Author 54

IV. Rothwell Console (Rothwell Patent Stop Control),
St. George's Chapel Royal, Windsor Castle . . 55

V. Rutt Console (Luminous Stop Keys), Church of St.
Martin-in-the-Fields, London 86

VI. Typical French Console by Cavaillé-Coll . . . 87

VII. Steinmeyer Console, Passau Cathedral, Germany . . 102

VIII. Town-hall Organ, Sydney, N.S.W. 103

IN THE TEXT

FIG.   PAGE
1. Organ Action 5

2. Drawstop Action 11

3. Stop Keys 18

PART ONE

ORGAN STOPS

CHAPTER I

THE ACTION OF THE STOP

THE word "stop" is employed somewhat loosely in organ terminology. Sometimes it is used as an abbreviation of drawstop knob, or stop key. Again, it is used for non-speaking or mechanical parts of the instrument, such as couplers, tremulants, and so on. More correctly it is used to describe the complete set of pipes comprising one unit of organ tone, e.g. diapason, gamba, flute, trumpet, etc. Historically, and strictly speaking, a stop is the complete mechanism which literally "stops" any given rank of pipes from sounding, until desired by the player. In the case of mixtures, the mechanism "stops" several ranks from sounding. Before the invention of stops, early in the fifteenth century, *all ranks*, or "full organ" was heard every time a key was depressed.

To-day, we think of stops rather as the means by which we *add* power, or obtain variety in the tone of the instrument as heard during performance. We also differentiate between sounding stops, and non-sounding stops. Thus, we speak of an organ (say that in York Minster) as possessing 73 speaking stops, and 22 couplers, etc., making a total of 95 registers.

A good deal of confusion would be saved if the use of the word "stop" was confined to speaking registers only, excluding couplers and other mechanical devices.

The word "register" is interesting. It is often interchangeable with the word "stop," and is said to have been derived from the slider (described below) which *registers* or regulates the number of pipes permitted to sound at any one time. From this word is derived the term "registration," which is the main subject of this book, and which in organ terminology means the use, control, and management of all the stops, couplers, and other mechanical devices, except the actual keyboards, manual and pedal, and of course the blower.

Travelling up and down the country lecturing to organists and enthusiasts on organ construction, I have found that many players had only very hazy ideas as to how their instrument functions. All, of course, know that there are pipes, wind supply, and some mysterious connecting mechanism called "action." This is unfortunate, for, while to the organist music is of much more importance than mechanism, the player who has at least a general idea of the working principles of the organ will certainly find this knowledge both helpful and interesting, as I have proved on many occasions. Mechanism, however, is the means; music the end. After all, except for the pipes, the organ is just a complicated wind-distributing machine. In order to assist the reader in this matter I have prepared some simple diagrams which will, I hope, set forth the working principles underlying the three main types of organ action in use to-day. In order to avoid obscurity I have ruthlessly omitted many purely technical details, and have exaggerated the relative proportions of moving parts so as to bring them into greater prominence.

TRACKER ACTION

Fig. 1 represents (in end section) the key action for one note, on the mechanical, tubular-pneumatic (pressure or supply), and electro-pneumatic systems respectively. This mechanism is multiplied sixty-one times for the manual compass of five octaves. Each pipe shown represents just *one* out of a complete rank of sixty-one.

To consider the key action first. The drawing on the left over A depicts mechanical action. When in use the wind chest, WCh (often called the soundboard), is charged with pressure wind. The key, K, is just a simple lever of the first order, and if the front end is depressed by the finger, the back

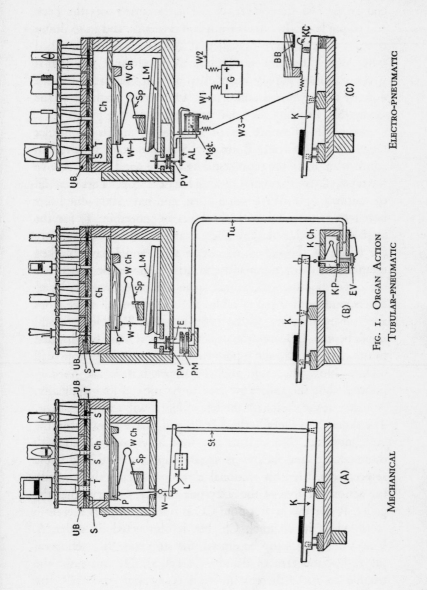

Fig. 1. Organ Action

Mechanical   Tubular-pneumatic   Electro-pneumatic

end rising lifts the sticker, St. This in turn raises the back
end of the lever, L, whose front end descends, and in so doing
opens the large valve or pallet, P, by means of the attached
wire, W. Thus wind is admitted to the channel, Ch, which
is the common supply channel to all stops actuated by one
note of the keyboard concerned. On release of the key, the
spring, Sp, aided by the wind pressure, closes the pallet, P.

Above the complete set of sixty-one channels is the flat
table, T, through which are bored all the holes required to
admit wind to all the pipes standing on the wind chest. Above
the table, T, are the sliders, S, one for each stop. These extend
the entire length of the wind chest, and have sixty-one holes
bored to correspond with the holes in the table, T, for the
stops concerned. As the sketch is an end cross-section, only
the width of the sliders, S, can be seen, and I have blacked
them in, to show them more clearly. Above the sliders are
the upper boards, UB, which again are bored with holes to
correspond with those in table, T. As shown, all three stops
are "on"; therefore all the holes in table, T, sliders, S, and
upper boards, UB, are in alignment. Thus, if wind be admitted
to the channel, Ch, the pipes belonging to the three stops will
sound. Now the table and the upper boards are *fixed* in
position, but the sliders are free to be moved longitudinally.
A glance at the sketch on the left of Fig. 2 will make this clear.
The slider, S, is literally the STOP, and I have drawn it in the
"off" position. None of its sixty-one holes corresponds with
those above and below it in the upper board and table
respectively. (In this sectional elevation I have shown only
the action for five of the sixty-one notes.) Observe that the
pallet, P, for the lowest note CC is open. Wind is therefore
admitted to its channel, Ch, but is obstructed by slider, S.
If now the stop knob be drawn, the stop rod, SR, acting on
the right-hand arm of trundle (or roller), Tr, will cause the
trundle to turn, thereby moving connecting rod, CR, by
means of the left-hand arm. CR will simultaneously draw

slider, S, into the "on" position through stop lever, SL. This will bring all the sixty-one holes in the slider into alignment with those in table, T, and upper boards, UB. A free passage for the wind, therefore, is opened between the channels and the pipes, enabling them to sound whenever their respective channels are charged with wind by the opening of the pallets concerned.

THE PNEUMATIC LEVER

One of the greatest events in the annals of organ building was the invention of the pneumatic lever. This is generally attributed to Charles Spackman Barker of Bath, but it is also claimed that David Hamilton of Edinburgh was first in the field. At any rate the action came to be known as Barker-Lever action. Barker collaborated with the great French organ builder, Aristide Cavaillé-Coll, and many of the noblest French instruments are still operated upon this fine (but sometimes noisy) system. Later, in England, pneumatic-lever action was brought to its highest degree of excellence in the ingenious floating pneumatic lever of Vincent Willis. A few fine examples of this mechanism still exist, e.g. Truro Cathedral, Cornwall. In this action the motion of the pallet coincides with that of the key (as in the ordinary tracker action just described) instead of opening *fully* on slightly depressing it. Pneumatic-lever action, including the floating pneumatic lever, however, is really obsolete in England and America, and almost so on the continent of Europe. For this reason, I have not included a diagram of this system. The basic principle underlying the pneumatic lever is that of overcoming the pressure of wind on the pallets and of their springs, by means of wind pressure acting upon a motor bellows of much larger surface area.

TUBULAR AND ELECTRO-PNEUMATIC ACTIONS

This same principle is in use to-day in modern tubular and electro-pneumatic actions, but the wind pressure acts upon the outside of the motor bellows inversely. In the Barker-Lever action the wind acted inside, and inflated the motor bellows, expanding them and so operating the action. In present-day action the wind pressure deflates and collapses them. A glance at the central sketch, over B, in Fig. 1, will make this clear. When in use, wind chest, WCh, and key chest, KCh, are both charged with pressure wind. If the key, K, be depressed, the back end rises, and opens the key pallet, KP. In the sketch a small plunger rod (unlettered) is shown holding open the exhaust valve, EV, against its light spring. On the key pallet being lifted, this spring promptly closes EV. Thus pressure wind can now proceed up the tube, Tu, and so inflate the small primary motor, PM, which rises and closes primary valve, PV. Now wind has been entering the long motor (bellows), LM, via the little channel in which PV moves, and so equalizing the pressure within and without long motor, LM; but as soon as PV closes, wind is shut off from the interior of LM. The wind pressure in WCh, acting upon the large outer surface of LM, instantly compresses that motor, which consequently opens pallet, P, by means of wire, W. It should be noticed that the lifting of primary valve, PV, not only closes wind from within LM, but also opens exhaust, E, thus instantly relieving LM of internal wind pressure. On release of the key, the little key pallet, KP, is closed by its spring, and exhaust valve, EV, is opened again. Primary motor, PM, now descends, causing primary valve, PV, to close exhaust, E, and admit wind to the interior of long motor, LM. Pressure now being equalized both within and without LM, the spring, Sp, plus wind pressure closes pallet P. This system is known as the " pressure or supply system."

There is another form of tubular action called the "exhaust system," in which the primary motors are supplied with wind when at *rest*, which proceeds *from* them along the tubes to the key pallets. The key opens the key pallet, and so *exhausts* the primary motor, which brings about precisely the same cycle of movements within the wind chest as above described.

The sketch over C, on the right of Fig. 1, shows a modern form of electro-pneumatic action.

Electric organ action depends entirely on the principle of the electro-magnet, which is as follows—

If a core of soft iron be wound round by numerous spiral coils of insulated wire, it will become a magnet during the passage of an electric current through the coils of wire. The magnet will attract an iron armature, releasing it when the current is cut off. Such an electro-magnet will be seen lettered Mgt in my sketch. The current generator, G, is permanently connected with Mgt from its (−) terminal by wire, W1. The bus-bar, BB, is similarly associated with the (+) terminal of supply by wire, W2; key contact, KC, being joined to the other end of the coil of Mgt by wire, W3. If, therefore, the key, K, be depressed, its back end will rise and bring key contact, KC, in touch with bus-bar, BB. The circuit is now completed. The electric current proceeds from generator, G, along W2, to bus-bar, BB, thence via key contact, KC, and wire, W3, to the coils of magnet Mgt, and returns to the generator by wire W1. Thus, the central core of soft iron becomes a magnet which draws down the hooked end of armature lever, AL. The opposite end of AL rises, thereby closing primary valve, PV, and opening the exhaust port beneath it. Long motor, LM, is thereby deprived of internal wind pressure, and the pressure upon its outer surface causes it to collapse and draw open pallet, P, by means of wire, W. Immediately the key is released the electrical circuit is broken, magnet, Mgt, releases armature lever, AL, primary valve, PV, descends and so admits wind to the inside of long motor, LM, and pallet, P, is closed by the spring, Sp, and the wind pressure in the chest.

The pull and holding power of the type of magnet illustrated is quite remarkable, and some builders employ it to open single pipe-valves, and to operate multiple contacts and switches, without having recourse to wind pressure at all. This method is known as "direct electric action." Many builders, however, follow the Hope-Jones plan, and use small horse-shoe magnets with tiny armature valves for controlling the *primary* pneumatics. These little armature valves function in precisely the same way as primary valve, PV. The voltage employed for organ action is rarely more than 10–15 volts D.C. Before leaving the sketches of action work, it may be remarked that the two *outer* stops are "off" in the central drawing, and likewise the two *rear* stops in the right-hand sketch.

THE PIPES

It is, I think, desirable that the player should have at least a nodding acquaintance with the appearance of the pipes of the more important stops, and also some idea how they function. For this purpose, I have devoted the bulk of Fig. 2 to illustrations showing the more usual forms of flue pipes (A to G), reeds (H to M), and diaphones N and O. With the exception of the pipe lettered G, all the pipes are drawn approximately to scale for the lowest note of the stop concerned. We will deal with the flue pipes first.

The pipe lettered A represents the large open diapason CC (or 8 ft C). It is tuned by means of the slot and tongue at the top of the pipe in the drawing. The same pipe is shown in section, lettered B. The principal 4 ft pipe, and fifteenth 2 ft pipe, are lettered C and D respectively. Notice the bayleaf form of mouth, as compared with the French mouth of the 8 ft diapason. The pipe lettered F is the small-scaled viole d'orchestre.

This, like the principal and fifteenth, is tuned by a sliding cylindrical metal shade at the top of the pipe. In the viole there is a long slot near the top of the pipe, which is partly covered by the shade. Observe the roller in front of the mouth attached to the projections called the ears of the pipe.

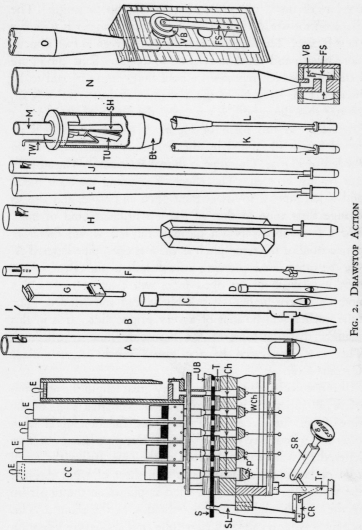

Fig. 2. Drawstop Action

A-G The Pipes: "Flue-pipes"; H-M "Reed Pipes"; N, O "Diaphones"

The word "scale," as applied to open pipes, denotes, in the case of metal pipes, diameter in relation to length. The diapason shown (A) is 6 in. scale, i.e. the diameter is 6 in. for the 8 ft pipe. The scale for wood pipes is given in two dimensions, width and depth in relation to length. Thus, the figure lettered G, which represents a hohl flute, might be said to be in scale 3 in. by 2 in. at the 2 ft pipe, or just 3 in. $\times$ 2 in. Notice that the mouth is cut upon the inside of the pipe, or "inverted" as this form of mouth is called. A large scale wood bass is illustrated by the five pipes under letter E, on the left of Fig. 2. One pipe is shown in section. The stopper can readily be seen. The effect of stopping on both metal and wood pipes is to lower their pitch an octave, and also to change their tone to that of the less brilliant kind of flute. The 4 ft stopped pipe on the extreme left would therefore give a note of the same pitch as the 8 ft open pipe lettered A. On the other hand, piercing a small hole in the centre of the speaking length of an open pipe, will cause it to sound a note an octave higher—if suitably voiced and winded. The tone quality will be that of a very bright flute. It is in this manner that the tone of the harmonic flute is obtained. This was discovered by the great French organ builder Cavaillé-Coll.

It is not necessary to discuss at any great length the acoustics of organ pipes. It may, however, be said that each of the three types, flues, reeds, and diaphones, function upon what is termed a "coupled system." In the flue pipe (see the section lettered B) wind enters the foot of the pipe, strikes the metal roof or languid, and issues in a thin sheet of wind through the windway. This sheet of wind impinges on the upper lip of the mouth, and so sets up vibration at the mouth. This produces what is called an edge tone, and also sets in vibration the column of air in the pipe (or resonator) above. It is the union of these two effects which forms the coupled system, and it is the voicer's business to bring these two factors into correct relationship, in order to produce the desired tone quality.

In the reed pipe the vibrations are first set up by the tongue in the boot of the pipe. The figure lettered M (towards the top right-hand of Fig. 2) shows a reed boot, cut away so as to disclose the vibratory mechanism.

The brass tongue, TU, curves away from the orifice in the flattened face of a small brass tube (or shallot) SH, at its lower end. When wind enters the boot, Bt, it rushes past the edges of the tongue into the shallot. This results in the formation of a partial vacuum behind the tongue, which enables the wind pressure almost to close it over the shallot. The flow of wind into the shallot is thus checked, and the partial vacuum is relieved. This allows the resiliency (or spring) of the tongue to open it again, and at once, the cycle of movements is repeated, and continues until the wind is shut off by the closing of the pallet. Thus, the vibrations are started at the tongue. These pulsations set the air column of the tube (or resonator) in vibration. Once again we have a coupled system, in this case between the tongue and the air column. Both factors have great influence upon the tone quality of reed pipes. Notice the tuning wire, TW, for lengthening or shortening the vibrating portion of the tongue.

The sketches of reed pipes are drawn to the same scale as the open diapason, A. The noble proportions of the mitred pedal ophicleide, or trombone for 16 ft CCC, are shown at letter H. The trumpet 8 ft is depicted at letter I. The pipes of the tuba are of the same form as the trumpet, but differ in scale. The thin-toned solo orchestral oboe is shown lettered J, for the same note, and likewise the clarinet at letter K. The clarinet is a half-length stop, i.e. a 4 ft tube for 8 ft CC. The pipe represented at letter L is the much over-used swell oboe for 4 ft C. The bell and its shade on the top should be noticed.

Letters N and O illustrate two forms of diaphone pipes. The former is typical of the large-scale diaphonic bass, the latter represents the smaller diaphone bass. The diaphone was introduced, and may have been invented in its present form, by Robert Hope-Jones. It has not found very much favour, but at its best, as developed by the John Compton Organ Company, it is of very great value, chiefly in the bass register. There is a noble example at 32 ft pitch in the Pavilion, Bournemouth, and an even finer one of the same pitch in the Compton organ at Southampton Civic Centre. In fairness to the memory of Hope-Jones it should be mentioned that his 32 ft diaphone in the roof of M'Ewan Hall, Edinburgh, still functions well, apart from some little irregularity. My sketches illustrate the Compton type of diaphone and chest, with the vibrator and box in section (N) and an enlargement of the vibrator, VB, under letter O. Wind enters the vibrator box in the direction indicated by the arrow, and rushes round the vibrator valve or disc, VB, and into the resonator, N. As with the tongue of the reed, this sets up a partial vacuum behind VB, and the wind pressure acting upon the large surface of VB overcomes the flat spring, FS, to which it is attached, and almost closes the orifice behind VB. At once the rarification behind VB ceases, and atmospheric pressure is restored. This enables the flat spring, FS, to re-open VB, which, of course, again results in a partial vacuum, and thus the cycle of events continues as long as the note is sounding. In this manner, wind is admitted to the resonator or tube in a series of very strong puffs, setting up a similarly strong vibration of the air column in the tube. Great power and sonority are obtainable by this means. Obviously, diaphones operate as a similar coupled system to that of the reeds.

The reader who has mastered these explanations of the action, pipework, and elementary acoustics of the organ has acquired, at any rate, a knowledge of the basic principles underlying the instrument. He will find that the most complicated mechanism of the large modern organ offers immense variety in the application of these principles, as applied to key action, drawstop action, combination action, etc. As will be realized, the number of working parts in a large instrument is very considerable, and may readily amount to several thousands. Many builders have discarded the slider wind chest as here described, substituting a type of chest in which a small valve is provided for each individual pipe. There are many forms of "sliderless" chest, and some of them are rather difficult for the layman to understand. The slider chest, however, is still used by a number of the most eminent organ builders of the present day.

Readers desiring a more detailed knowledge of the various forms of wind chest, or of the complete mechanism of the modern organ, its pipework, and acoustics, will find these matters fully described and illustrated in *The Electric Organ* (3rd edition) by the present writer.

CHAPTER II

THE STOP KEY

IT is impossible to say with certainty who invented the "stop key," a term somewhat loosely used to indicate methods of control of individual registers, other than the traditional stop knob. Sometimes we read that Hope-Jones was the originator of the idea, but this is extremely improbable. There is a good reason for believing that this form of control was in use on the Continent long before that remarkable genius appeared. The writer once played an organ in Belgium where the stops were actuated by keys of the same type as those for the manuals, which are placed between the sharps, viz. D, G, A. These keys projected through terraced jambs with a hitch-down movement of about $\frac{5}{8}$ in., similar in principle to the old-fashioned lever swell pedal, but on a diminutive scale. When hitched *down*, the stop was "on." When released, a fairly strong spring raised the key, and the register was put "off." Unquestionably this organ existed for many years anterior to Hope-Jones, and it may be that the designation "stop key" was originally derived from some such control. I have found only one such instance in England. This was by Brindley and Foster. The device resembled an ordinary keyboard, but with an equal number of white naturals and black sharps. The former, when depressed, remained so, thus maintaining the stop "on." A touch on the corresponding sharp key released the white key which promptly returned to the "off" position.

It cannot be denied, however, that when Hope-Jones introduced his stop keys at St. John's Church, Birkenhead, in 1887, they came to stay, and as all players are not necessarily familiar with the several varieties used in England to-day, I have made a composite sketch, Fig. 3, illustrating the more important forms which have been evolved.

Under letter A will be seen a drawing of the tilting tablet control shown in elevation and section. This is the modern version of the ingenious, but rather small tablet used by Hope-Jones. Generally speaking, they are tilted forward for the "on" position (as shown), but Hope-Jones employed the reverse movement, and some builders still employ the backward tilt for the "on" position. This lack of standardization is unfortunate and confusing, as I have proved when playing, to my cost. Under D, the admirable example used by the present firm of Willis is shown. Note the ends of the tablets, so shaped as to prevent the accidental catching of those on either side of the one operated. The figure below B represents the lever stop key. Again, this is the modern form of the Hope-Jones type, which superseded his tilting tablets. Several builders have made slight modifications in the length and pattern of their lever stop keys. The most notable is the Walker variety, the back portion of which is raised at an angle, in order that the engraving of the name and pitch may be easily seen.

The very convenient tablets of the Conacher firm are depicted under C. These have an up-and-down movement, the latter being the "on" position. Under letters E and F will be seen drawings of stop keys invented by Hele & Co. of Plymouth, and Rothwell of Harrow, respectively. In both instances, these are placed on the keyslip above the manual to which they belong. It is thus possible to make stop changes without removing the hands from the keyboards concerned. The Hele tablets have a rocking movement; the suboctave is thus shown. This is the "on" position, the level keys being "off." The form of the tablets in section is shown on the right. On the larger Hele stop-key consoles, the tablets for the pedal organ are duplicated right and left, on sloping jambs carried by the key cheeks.

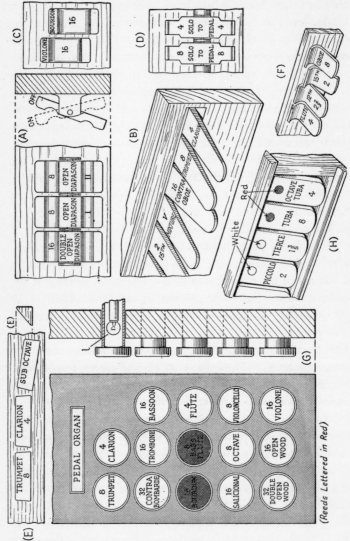

FIG. 3. STOP KEYS

(Reeds Lettered in Red)

The tablets for the pedal department of the Rothwell instrument are triplicated in their three- and four-manual consoles. They are placed over the choir, great, and swell keyboards respectively, to the left of the stop keys for the manual concerned. Thus, the pedal organ can be controlled while playing on any keyboard. Even if playing on the solo manual, the thumb can reach the pedal-organ tablets over the swell keys, and the cunning shape of the back ends of these stop keys enables the thumb to put the stops "off" with the same ease as they are put "on." This is a very real advantage, as in like manner all the tablets for their respective manual departments can readily be operated from the keyboard above.

LUMINOUS STOP CONTROL

The figure over G represents the form of luminous stop control as perfected by the Compton Organ Company, and used in many of their important instruments. Instead of draw knobs, round touches or pistons are substituted. The heads of these touches are made of translucent material, and on them the names of the stops and their pitch are clearly engraved. Within the barrel of each is placed a low-voltage electric lamp (lettered *l* in the sectional sketch on the right). When any stop is "on" its lamp glows, lighting up the piston head, but not causing a distracting glare. The stops are put "on" or "off" by pressing the pistons which have a movement of about $\frac{3}{16}$ in. The operation is precisely the same in each case, for the pistons have reversible action. If the stop is "on," pressure of the piston will put it "off," and vice versa. Second-touch cancelling (as described later) is also applied to these touches and a further pressure against a strong spring cancels any other stop in the department which may be "on," and therefore glowing. The pistons are grouped departmentally on raised panels, and as will be seen from my sketch are very economical in so far as space on the jambs

is concerned. It will be observed that the full pedal is represented as being "on." Notice that the bourdon 16 ft and bass
flute 8 ft are silent and therefore dark.

The figure over H depicts the luminous touches made by
Robert Spurden Rutt. Each tablet is hinged at the top. A
slight pressure on the lower portion operates a clever revers-
ing mechanism, and so puts the stop and the light "on" or
"off," as desired. Each lamp glows through a small bulbous
projection near the top of the tablet. These projections are
coloured red for reeds, white for flues, and green for couplers.

The idea of a colour scheme for stop keys was exploited
by Hope-Jones.

One very real advantage of the luminous control is
absolute silence of operation at the console. Vast registra-
tional changes involving the whole organ can be effected by
the combination pistons, etc., but as these only put "on"
or extinguish the lights, so far as the console is concerned,
no noise whatever is heard.

A description (with diagram) of this mechanism, and other
details of English and continental stop keys, will be found in
the author's book *The Electric Organ* (3rd edition).

CHAPTER III

THE STOPS TO BE FOUND IN BRITISH ORGANS

THE description of the tone quality of organ stops in words which will convey to the reader the precise aural impression such stops made upon the writers concerned, has proved an almost insurmountable difficulty to all writers about organ matters (not excluding the present author). Some writers use the most extravagant adjectives overflowing with superlatives. Indeed one writer described the tonal effect of a dulciana (almost the softest stop in the organ) as "terrific!"

In the list which follows I have tried to use few and simple words which will, I hope, readily be understood. The words "string" or "string tone" refer to the likeness of the tone quality to that of the orchestral family of strings, i.e. violins, violas, violoncellos, and contra basses, however slight or marked the resemblance may be. Incidentally, the name "contra bass" is found occasionally on organ stops of the pedal organ, which should be labelled "open wood," and which possess no trace of string tone whatever. It is also used sometimes for the Compton diaphonic bass.

I was much tempted to include in the list which follows the nearest continental equivalents to the British stops tabulated, but the great variety of tone quality and power which exist even in organ stops of the same name both at home and abroad made me decide against this procedure. The matter is dealt with, however, in later chapters.

Every organ has its own individuality which is largely affected by the acoustics of its environment.

GENERAL LIST OF ORGAN STOPS FOUND IN BRITISH ORGANS

I. FLUE STOPS (A. Open Pipes)

Pitch in ft	Name	Materials	Form of Pipes	Brief Tonal Characteristics
32	Double open diapason (pedal) .	Metal	Cylindrical	This group represents the true organ chorus, which imparts that dignified and sonorous effect at once recognizable as "organ tone," and which is produced by no other instrument
16	Double open diapason (manual) .	,,	,,	
8	Open diapason	,,	,,	
5⅓	Quint	,,	,,	
4	Octave, octave diapason, or principal	,,	,,	
2⅔	Twelfth	,,	,,	
2	Fifteenth, or super octave . .	,,	,,	Diapasons vary in quality and power, the higher ranks affording great brilliance to the ensemble
1⅗	Tierce, or seventeenth . . .	,,	,,	
Various	Compound stops of 2 to 10 ranks, such as mixture, sesquialtera, harmonics, acuta, etc. . . .	,,	,,	
32	Double open wood . . .	Wood	Rectangular with mouth on narrow side	Pedal stops of great weight and dignity
16	Open wood, major bass, or great bass .	,,	,,	
8	Octave wood	,,	,,	
21⅓	Double quint	Wood or metal	Rectangular or cylindrical	Pedal mutation stops of diapason or bourdon tone. If the latter, the pipes are "stopped"
10⅔	Quint	,,	,,	

Pitch in ft	Name	Materials	Form of Pipes	Brief Tonal Characteristics
32	Contra violone	Wood or metal	Rectangular or Cylindrical	Small diapasons voiced with a certain amount of string tone, varying according to the builder
16	Violone	,,	Cylindrical	
8	Viola	Metal	,,	
8	Violin diapason	,,	,,	
4	Octave viola	,,	,,	
4	Salicet	,,	,,	
16	Contra bass	,,	Cylindrical with rollers or beards	Fairly powerful, keen and imitative of orchestral strings
8	Violoncello	,,	,,	
4	Viola	,,	,,	
16	Gross, or contra geigen . .	,,	Cylindrical	About midway between a diapason and a gamba in tone and scale
8	Geigen	,,	,,	
4	Octave geigen, or geigen principal	,,	,,	
8	Spitzflöte	,,	Tapered pipes	Quiet silvery diapasons. Gemshorns are also made in 16 ft and 8 ft pitch in America. The upper portion of the 2 ft member has cylindrical pipes
4	Gemshorn. . . .	,,	,,	
2	Gemshorn. . . .	,,	,,	
16	Contra dulciana	,,	Cylindrical	Quiet, somewhat dull tone, sometimes slightly stringy in quality. The 8 ft stop is occasionally called echo diapason
8	Dulciana	,,	,,	
4	Dulcet, or dulcet principal .	,,	,,	
2⅔	Dulcet twelfth	,,	,,	
2	Dulcet fifteenth	,,	,,	

Pitch in ft	Name	Materials	Form of Pipes	Brief Tonal Characteristics
16	Salicional	Generally spotted metal	Rather small-scaled cylindrical	Less soft than the dulciana family, and also definitely more stringy. They form the mildest section of actual organ string tone
8	Salicional	,,	,,	
4	Salicional	,,	,,	
2	Salicional	,,	,,	
8	Aeoline	,,	,,	
8	Viol d'amour	,,	,,	
16	Contra gamba	,,	Small-scale cylindrical. Bearded and slotted near the top	Fairly keen string tone
8	Viol da gamba	,,	,,	
4	Octave gamba	,,	,,	
16	Contra viole	Metal, sometimes pure tin	Very small scale, cylindrical, bearded, and slotted near top	Extremely keen, very imitative of the strings of the orchestra
8	Viol d'orchestre	,,	,,	
4	Octave viole	,,	,,	
2	Viol fifteenth	,,	,,	
Various	Cornet violes, 2 to 5 ranks (string mixture)	,,	,,	

Pitch in ft	Name	Materials	Form of Pipes	Brief Tonal Characteristics
1⅗	Tierce	Metal	Medium-scaled cylindrical or tapered pipes	Mutation stops, varying in tone quality according to their purpose and make
1⅓	Larigot or octave 12th	"	"	
1⅐	Septime	"	"	
8	Hohl flöte	Wood or metal	Rectangular or cylindrical, mouths often "inverted" on wider side of wood pipes	Fairly loud open flute
8	Clarabella or claribel	Wood	"	
8	Wald flute	"	"	Clear soft open flute (occasionally made of metal)
4	Wald flute	"	"	
4	Suabe flute	"	"	
4	Concert flute	Wood or metal	"	Bright clear flute (sometimes "harmonic")
8	Harmonic flute	Metal	Pipes of double length, pierced in centre, and blown to sound octave	Very bright flute
4	Harmonic flute	"	"	
2	Harmonic piccolo	"	"	
1	Piccolo	Cylindrical	"	Sometimes harmonic; bright flute tone
8	Flute triangulaire	Wood	Triangular pipes	Beautiful, fairly quiet flute

FLUE STOPS (B. Stopped Pipes—Half Length)

Pitch in ft	Name	Materials	Form of Pipes	Brief Tonal Characteristics
32	Contra bourdon	Wood	Large-scale rectangular	Pedal bass of dull flute tone, very pervading in lower octaves
16	Bourdon or sub bass	,,	,,	Manual or pedal, as above but softer
16	Echo bourdon, or lieblich bourdon	,,	Smaller scale rectangular	
8	Tibia clausa	Wood or metal	Very large scale	A huge "cloying" flute
8	Stopped diapason	,,	Medium scale	Rather dull flute tone
8	Rohr flöte	,,	Pierced stoppers	
8	Lieblich gedeckt	,,	Rather small-scale pipes	Quiet liquid flute tone
4	Lieblich flöte	,,	,,	
2	Lieblich piccolo	,,	,,	
2⅔	Nazard	,,	Medium scale	A valuable mutation stop of gedeckt tone
8 or 4	Harmonic gedeckt	,,	Pierced stopped pipes	A clear flute sometimes called by its makers zauberflöte
16	Quintaton	,,	Rather large-scale stopped pipes	The pipes are voiced to sound their ground tone and twelfth together, in about equal power (very occasionally found in 32 ft pitch on the manuals, e.g. St. Nicholas's Church, Whitehaven)
8	Quintaton	,,	,,	
4	Quintadena	,,	,,	

FLUE STOPS (C. Undulating Stops)

Pitch in ft	Name						Materials	Form of Pipes	Brief Tonal Characteristics
8	Violes célestes	.	.	.	.	.	Metal, often spotted metal or pure tin	Very small scale, slotted and bearded	Very keen string tone. Tuned sharp
8	Voix célestes	.	.	.	.	.	,,	Rather larger scale	Gamba tone, less keen than above, tuned sharp
8	Unda maris	.	.	.	.	.	,,	Salicional, dulciana or flute pipes	Mild string tone or flute, generally tuned flat to the parent rank. Sometimes 2 ranks
8	Vox angelica	.	.	.	.	.	,,	Mild string or dulciana	Very soft. Sometimes tuned sharp, flat or dead
8	Flute céleste	.	.	.	.	.	Wood or metal	Stopped or open pipes	Flutes tuned sharp or flat (occasionally labelled Unda maris)

N.B. The above five stops are tuned *slightly* sharp or flat to their parent rank, viole d'orchestre, viol da gamba, salicional, dulciana or flute. This results in a very pleasant waving effect, which, however, should be sparingly used, as it becomes wearisome if employed too frequently.

2. REED STOPS

Pitch in ft	Name	Materials	Form of Pipes	Brief Tonal Characteristics
32	Contra bombarde . . .	Wood or metal	Large scale	Very powerful pedal reeds of trumpet or tromba tone
32	Contra trombone . . .	,,	,,	
32	Contra posaune . . .	,,	,,	
32	Double ophicleide . .	Metal	,,	
16	Trombone, bombarde .	Wood or metal	,,	
16	Ophicleide . . .	Metal	,,	
32	Contra fagotto (pedal)	Wood or metal	Small scale	Pedal reeds of fairly soft bassoon tone
16	Fagotto or double bassoon	,,	,,	
16	Trombone, double trumpet	Metal	Medium scale	Trumpet-toned chorus reeds of fiery quality. Upper octaves generally "harmonic" (double length)
16	Contra posaune . .	,,	,,	
8	Harmonic trumpet . .	,,	,,	
8	Trumpet, posaune . .	,,	,,	
4	Clarion . . .	,,	,,	
16	Waldhorn, contra fagotto .	,,	Smaller scale	Less fiery reeds, upper octaves often "harmonic" generally placed on swell
8	Horn, cornopean . .	,,	,,	
16	Contra oboe . . .	,,	Small scale with bells and shades	Quiet, non-imitative foundational tone
8	Oboe . . .	,,	,,	
4	Oboe clarion, octave oboe .	,,	,,	
16	Contra tromba . . .	,,	Moderate scale	Powerful chorus reeds of moderately smooth tonality. Generally "harmonic" in upper octaves
8	Tromba . . .	,,	,,	
4	Octave tromba . .	,,	,,	

Pitch in ft	Name	Materials	Form of Pipes	Brief Tonal Characteristics
16	Contra tuba	Metal	Medium or large scale	Very powerful, fairly smooth, but brilliant tone. Generally "harmonic" in upper octaves. Always placed on heavy wind
8	Tuba	”	”	
4	Tuba clarion, or octave tuba	”	”	
8	Trompette militaire	”	Spun brass tubes with "flared" bells	Powerful cavalry trumpet tone
16	Cor anglais	”	Tubes have imitation globular bells	
8	Cor anglais	”	Very small scale	Closely imitative of their orchestral prototypes
8	Orchestral oboe	”	”	
16	Contra (or double) clarinet	”	Half-length cylindrical tubes	
8	Clarinet, corno di bassetto	”	”	
8	French horn	”	Large scale	Often "harmonic" in upper octaves, imitative
16	Baryton	”	Very short tubes	Mock-pathetic quality, intended to imitate the human voice
8	Vox humana	”	”	

3. DIAPHONE STOPS

Pitch in ft	Name				Materials	Form of Pipes	Brief Tonal Characteristics
32	Diaphonic horn	.	.	.	Wood or metal	Very large scale	Very full foundational rather reedy quality
16	Diaphonic horn	.	.	.	,,	,,	Powerful very weighty foundational tone
32	Diaphonic tibia bass	.	.	.	,,	,,	
8	Diaphonic diapason	.	.	.	,,	Large scale	Big diapason tone
16	Diaphonic violone	.	.	.	,,	Medium scale	Big violone quality

N.B. Diaphone pipes are occasionally used for the bass notes of several varieties of organ stops, particularly when these are placed in awkward positions which interfere with the egress of sound.

PART TWO

THE USE OF ORGAN STOPS

CHAPTER IV

DIAPASONS, FULL ORGAN, AND TUBAS

ERHAPS the art of combining organ stops, and of making the most of a small number of registers has received less attention in musical literature than the subject deserves. It is indeed important, but it is a subject upon which we cannot be unduly dogmatic. It has been well said that, "No two organs are precisely alike." In fact, it cannot be denied that a combination of stops used in one building with quite admirable results, may be grievously disappointing, though apparently the same on paper, in a different building.

This is not all to the bad, for do not these very differences help to give each instrument its own individuality?

Now one of the best effects in organ registration is the use of a single stop alone. We used to hear the late Sir Walter Parratt, and the late Dr. Kendrick Pyne of Manchester improvise, using one stop alone. To hear these great organists play trios with only one register drawn upon each manual, of contrasted tonality, with only an 8 ft pedal, was indeed an object lesson in organ technique! The swell pedal rarely used, nothing but meticulous phrasing, and true rhythm right from the opening in single notes. Sometimes, of course, this would lead up to a more powerful climax in which, however, phrasing, rhythm, and clarity always prevailed.

It is quite remarkable what an amount of expression can be obtained from even an unenclosed gedeckt by means of delicate phrasing. The art is not dead, as Dr. Thalben Ball so often proved at the Temple Church. Not a few others too, in our cathedrals and elsewhere, possess that great gift, and produce little gems of expressive organ playing from single stops.

This brings us to another point. How many organists really know the tone quality of each individual stop in the organ upon which they play week by week, or day by day? I wonder; and more important still its effect as heard in the church! Probably very few of us go through each stop separately from time to time, in order to ascertain what portion of its compass offers the most musical results. Yet many organ stops do vary in tonality in different regions. They are not *all* the perfect article. Some stops offer a bass and tenor section that is good to know, others a fine, well-regulated treble, others again a superb middle section. For example, I well remember the oboe stop of an organ upon which I used to play which had a remarkable middle section of about two octaves. I used to combine the 4 ft gemshorn with this, and so obtained a capital orchestral oboe. Above or below this particular section the effect simply did not come off, and one heard merely a very ordinary oboe, and easily recognized the gemshorn with it. What on earth is the good of all that, some people may ask. Just this: it was (within its limited compass) a new tone quality, very valuable on this comparatively small organ, useful alike in improvisation, and in quite a number of written organ pieces. Now if I had been content to stick to what my few composition pedals gave, plus a few stereotyped combinations, I should never have discovered this simple but valuable effect.

DIAPASONS

Diapasons played singly offer more subtle variety than many seem to realize. How often an organist, with only a fat diapason on the great of a two-manual organ, simply longs for a second smaller one. Well, he may find that he already possesses it, if he plays upon the 4 ft principal an octave lower. He may not, for it does not always work out suitably, but quite frequently he will obtain the desired result. Of course, the lowest octave is missing, but he may possibly be able to cover that defect. Where a double open diapason exists, it may be played an octave higher to produce the effect of a second, or even a third open diapason. In this case, it is the top octave that is missing. Mr. Norman Cocker (of Manchester Cathedral) is a past master in the art of using stops in pitches other than normal, and finds the practice well worth while even on larger organs. I seem to remember the late Dr. Madeley Richardson, when at Southwark Cathedral, making frequent use of a 4 ft flute in a different octave in order to get just the power and quality he desired, there being no flute of that precise type at the pitch required, large though this fine organ is.

As stated in the list of organ stops, the diapason chorus constitutes the main ingredient of true organ tone. In fact, it is just this clear and pervading quality, which is at once recognized as "organ tone." Where a really complete chorus exists, comprising (say) the following members,

Double open diapason .	. 16 ft	Principal	.	.	.	. 4 ft
Open diapason I .	. 8 ft	Twelfth	.	.	.	. 2⅔ ft
Open diapason II	. 8 ft	Fifteenth	.	.	.	. 2 ft
Open diapason III	. 8 ft	Seventeenth	.	.	.	1⅗ ft
Quint	. 5⅓ ft	Mixture	.	.	.	rks III
Octave	. 4 ft	Fourniture .	.	.		rks V

not only is the full diapason ensemble noble and inspiring, but several smaller contrasted ensembles can readily be compounded within the family. Again, the 16 ft member can be combined with either of the 8 ft stops, and played an octave higher, or these combinations may be played in normal pitch and enriched by the addition of one or both 4 ft members, to which the 2 ft may further be added if desired. The quint 5⅓ ft, and twelfth 2⅔ ft will give most valuable colour to these smaller ensembles if introduced at the appropriate moment. Great care, however, is needed in using the seventeenth 1⅗ ft, which will produce a reedy tang when added to the ensemble. Finally, the mixture and fourniture will each give individual colour to the ensemble of which they form, as it were, the crown. They will also greatly assist in combining the flue and reed choruses into a cohesive whole.

FULL SWELL

Again, consider the full swell. This is undoubtedly one of the glories of an English organ. It consists chiefly of chorus reeds 16—(8)—8—4 ft, principal 4 ft, and mixture III–V ranks (with a good clarion 4 ft, the principal may not be needed). Many full-swell pistons throw out every swell stop except those of the undulating or célestes type of register and vox humana, if such is present. Sometimes this may be satisfactory, but more often the result is thick in texture, and clarity of effect, especially in music containing moving inner parts, is completely sacrificed. This produces noise. Pleasant noise maybe, but confusion rather than music when the actual notes of the player cannot be distinguished. To the above recipe for a clear-toned full swell, the 8 ft diapason and even the 8 ft gamba may be added in some instances, but it is rarely advantageous, and to add flute tone, especially in 16 ft pitch, is definitely harmful.

Some of our younger organists may probably wonder how it comes about that in our cathedrals and larger churches the player seems to have at his command more than one type of full swell. This may be achieved by a judicious selection of stops and the use of the octave couplers. For example, I was once playing upon an admirable two-manual organ not far from Belfast, built by Evans and Barr of that city. On the swell was a capital rather free-toned contra fagotto 16 ft. I produced an excellent smaller full swell by using this 16 ft reed together with the open diapason 8 ft, mixture and octave coupler. The addition of the 8 ft reeds, still retaining the octave coupler, gave a more fiery type of full swell. I have found on occasion that a valuable miniature full-swell effect could be obtained by using the oboe, mixture and principal, together with sub-octave and octave couplers. This, of course, is limited in compass to the three octaves affected by both sub and octave couplers. It is much on these lines that our cathedral organists produce various ensembles suggestive of full swell. Generally too a 4 ft clarion is present, which again offers some intriguing effects to the experimenter.

FULL ORGAN

What has been said of full-swell effects is largely applicable to the full great and full organ. For many years (judging by the stops fixed on full-organ pedals and pistons) the term "full organ" has been taken in the most literal sense, only tremulants, undulating stops, and vox humana being omitted. I have seen even the quietest vox angelicas and dulcianas included in full organ, and, of course, all flutes, open or stopped.

It should be observed, that I am, in this chapter, writing of English instruments. Continental organ ensembles differ considerably, and flute tone often forms an integral part of their ensemble.

To-day there is a distinct call for clarity in the *tout ensemble*, and full effects which are unduly thick in texture, or in which it would be impossible to distinguish moving inner parts, should rarely (if ever) be used.

On a comparatively small organ a little experimentation will soon show which stops obscure the clarity of the full organ, and these should be allowed to remain quiescent. Often the culprits (if any) will be found to be the flutes, especially harmonic flutes, 16 ft bourdons, and couplers, both sub and octave, especially the former. A good deal depends upon the acoustics of the particular building, as well as upon the tone quality of the stops concerned. If an octave coupler really enhances the full effect, and quite a number do, it must not be used in music which ascends into the top octave of the keyboard. If this is overlooked the true treble line of the music will be destroyed, unless, as in most organs in America, the compass is extended upwards to 73 notes.

The sub octave used in full effects may add breadth and dignity, or more often it may produce muddle and growl! On the other hand I have found in some organs that a choir-to-great sub (used with most of the choir fluework) has added a valuable depth and richness, without destruction of clarity, not only to full organ, but also when used with the great diapason ensemble.

In extremely large instruments, and very resonant buildings, the full organ raises further points for consideration, and quite a number of lesser full effects are available on the lines indicated for the full swell. These are well worth the time and trouble taken in experiment and trial. Further, the speed at which any music can be played in order to retain its clarity in resonant buildings is a matter for serious consideration.

TUBAS

Then the question of the tuba, or the family of tubas. Is it permissible to couple these to the full organ?

Some authorities would prohibit this, or allow only a chord in either hand, or coupled to the pedal, or an octave to establish final key tonality. Personally, I agree with the many who consider that tubas may be coupled to the full great with advantage on rare occasions, both in recital work and when accompanying vast congregations, but not as a matter of course at the end of every loud piece. I have at times heard the famous dome tubas at St. Paul's Cathedral work wonders uncoupled, in leading mighty congregations in the singing of popular hymns. Coupling the tubas in octaves to the full great is rarely good, especially if there is a tuba clarion 4 ft present. Noise is generally the result.

A great deal, of course, depends upon the individual organ and its effect in the particular building. When accompanying a large concourse of people holding forth lustily, the tuba

Plate I. England's Largest Organ: Modern "Willis" Console, Liverpool Cathedral

(*By courtesy of Henry Willis & Sons Ltd., London*)

PLATE II. COMPTON CONSOLE (LUMINOUS STOP TOUCHES),
SOUTHAMPTON GUILDHALL

(*By courtesy of the John Compton Organ Co. Ltd., London*)

coupled to the pedal will tread out time, as it were, and help to keep the crowd together. A thrilling effect for occasional use can be obtained by playing the melody on the pedals with tuba coupled accompanied on the full great alone.

Not much need be said here of the use of the tuba as a solo stop, for it is generally indicated where required in copies of organ music. Its obvious success when used occasionally as a leader during the accompaniment of suitable lines in certain hymns should not mislead the young organist into making such a line for every hymn! Oh yes, this has been done. I have heard the gentlemen myself, also others who give us full organ for the last verse, regardless of the hymn concerned! The use of the tuba in chords alone in contrast to the full great flue work is often most thrilling.

A final word about full organ. Many recitalists would do well, when playing upon really large organs, to avoid the use of absolute full organ for the close of every loud piece in their programmes. On big instruments, lesser full effects will often produce the needful sense of climax in final cadences, and some variety will thus be maintained.

The organists in our cathedrals often teach as much in the matter of artistic restraint in the use of power in big organs. During a congress of organists, the late Dr. Harvey Grace made some very wise and pithy remarks on the subject of NOISE.

CHAPTER V

STRING TONE

UNDER this heading the large modern organ offers a considerable variety of stops, both in pitch and in power, and also in quality. These range tonally from the quiet salicional and vox angelica, sometimes having only just enough "bite" to escape being dulcianas (like some of the older Father Willis examples), to the keenest Hope-Jones type of viole; or in power from the merest whisper of an echo gamba, to the admirable powerful string tone in some of the Compton organs, or the fine broad examples of the present Henry Willis, found at the Alexandra Palace, London, and elsewhere. In pitch we have string tone to-day which ranges from 32 ft to string mixtures, a few of our organs possessing complete families of violes from 16 ft to mixture, such as those by the late Arthur Harrison in Ely Cathedral, and his later string choruses at Durham Cathedral, Westminster Abbey, and the Royal Albert Hall, or the modern Willis string chorus at Liverpool Cathedral.

The majority of organs, however, generally possess but a single gamba and voix céleste on the swell, a string-tone stop of some sort on the choir, and a violone 16 ft on the pedal. This latter may be a noble independent stop, moderately powerful, or it may be a keen, vigorous stop of the Willis contre bass type, a fine stop for giving definition in suitable pedal passages. Yet again, it may be the great double open diapason, which sometimes undergoes a change of title when borrowed for the pedal!

Manual string-toned stops may readily be over-used, not to say abused. There is a class of player who always softens down the organ after accompanying psalms and hymns, and invariably finishes on the swell gamba and voix célestes! This is an abuse. If it is really necessary to reduce the organ, and to cover up the sound of the sitting down of the congregation, the organ offers several other classes of tone quite suitable for this purpose. There is a real danger of sentimentalizing over our voix célestes. But what when the vox humana is so used? Believe me, this *does* happen. I have heard it so abused all too frequently.

String tone generally, and the célestes effects especially, need using with discretion. It is not an essential part of the organ ensemble. It forms a most valuable contrast to the true organ tone, and this is lost if the string effects are overused. Nevertheless, some gambas, salicionals, and even violes can be used in general ensemble. Only experiment on individual organs will show how far this may be acceptable. I have met with viola stops in one or two organs which utterly destroy the cohesion of their respective diapason choruses. Yet the organists concerned do not appear to have noticed the fact, and would not dream of omitting these stops from the diapason ensemble! This does not, of course, refer to the geigen, which blends admirably.

The use of string tone for solo effects, either alone or combined with other stops, is most valuable. Generally speaking, string stops on the solo organ are voiced with that end in view, but instances are not lacking where extremely quiet and restful strings are to be found in this department, which rather suggest an "echo" division. The tenor registor of solo string tone is often a great asset, and its accompaniment on the quieter strings of the swell gives an admirable quasi-string orchestral character to the music. The use of octave couplers, or combined pitches of string tone is very valuable if not overdone, and with the "unison off," sometimes produces a mysterious effect of real charm; but again not on all organs. Often the unison pitch may be supplied by using a suitable string on another manual, through the appropriate intermanual coupler. This admits of several variations in timbre, and if the octave extremes and unison are in separate swell-boxes, the power of either or both may be varied with good effect, the one dissolving into the other.

Good string tone frequently blends well with flute tone, more particularly if the latter be an octave above or below the string tone in pitch. This proves effective in both solo and harmonic use. There are organs, too, where string tone will combine happily with the imitative reeds of the wood-wind group, when dead in tune.

CHAPTER VI

IMITATIVE REEDS

Tʜɪs section of organ stops generally comprises the bassoon (or fagotto 8 ft), contra bassoon (or contra fagotto 16 ft), double clarinet 16 ft, clarinet 8 ft, orchestral oboe 8 ft, cor anglais 16 or 8 ft, corno di bassetto 8 ft, and French horn 8 ft. The truly imitative form of this latter stop was invented by Ernest M. Skinner in America, and has only of recent years been introduced into English organs, though Willis included a stop of that *name* in his organ in the Royal Albert Hall in 1872; as also did Abbott and Smith in the organ in St. Albans Cathedral. Tonally the modern French horn stop is amazingly like its orchestral prototype. Not only will it admit of solo use, and contrasted use in harmony, but it can quite well be employed as a quasi-orchestral double (through appropriate couplers).[1]

The reed stops bearing the names of orchestral wood-wind instruments are naturally most effectively used for solo purposes, and of course, submit to the use of tremulants quite agreeably, if this is not abused. If dead in tune they will blend as a rule with each other, in unison, or in octaves, where different pitches are available, or by the employment of octave couplers. The occasional use of imitative reeds in chords is valuable. Even the acid-sweet tones of the orchestral oboe may be so employed. The clarinet, if in a good swell-box, will stand much more prolonged usage in harmony than other stops of this group, and has indeed been used successfully as a swell foundation double reed. Imitative reeds blend well with flute-toned stops, especially in octaves (i.e. the flute sounding an octave above or below the imitative reed).

---

[1] The trompette militaire is also an imitative reed, but it is essentially a solo voice.

CHAPTER VII

FLUTE TONE

Flute-toned stops are roughly divided into two main classes, stopped flutes and open flutes. In pitch they range from 32 ft to 2 ft (or even occasionally 1 ft). Stopped flutes are essentially of duller tone than open flutes, which are comparatively bright. Both will blend well together however, and where a number of different types exist in various pitches, a few experiments will often reveal some fascinating combinations within the family.

For accompanimental use flutes may well be employed in combination with dulcianas, gemshorns, salicionals, gambas, and even violes. If the stops themselves or the couplers allow, variety may be obtained by combining the flute tone with string or other tone quality in contrasted octaves, e.g. gamba 8 ft with flute 4 ft, or flute 8 ft with viole 4 ft, etc.

Large combinations or ensembles of soft stops may well include 16, 8, 4, and 2 ft flutes, but it is well to remember that stopped flutes like the stopped diapason, gedeckt, or rohr flöte blend more readily than open flutes. Harmonic flutes sometimes will not blend.

Clarity is essential. If your combination of stops, however pleasing, does not reveal your music, especially the inner parts, to the listener away from the organ, then your combination needs clarifying. For this reason, as a general rule, NEVER USE FLUTES WITH DIAPASONS. There are exceptions, however. The 16 ft stopped flute (or bourdon) may be your only great double, and in this pitch it frequently blends well; but even this must be removed whilst playing a fugal entry, otherwise it may sound like a gruff bass voice singing an octave below the pitch in a hymn or chant. Doubles, especially reeds, should be avoided in playing fugal music wherever their use would interfere with the correct hearing of the fugal structure. It is, however, the big hohl flötes and harmonic flutes that upset the English diapasons, rather than the stopped flutes. In some of our larger organs a quint $5\frac{1}{3}$ ft (of stopped flute pipes) will be found. These stops if introduced at the right moment in building up the great diapason chorus, will actually help to bind the various pitches into a clear and cohesive ensemble. Unfortunately we have all too few $5\frac{1}{3}$ ft quints in England; they belong to the harmonics of the 16 ft series.

Naturally flutes make admirable solo stops, and they take the tremulant well. Care must be taken, however, not to over-use the tremulant, either with flutes or other stops. There is a danger of aping the cinema organ effects. The big-scaled cloying flute, or tibia clausa of the cinema instrument, however, is rarely present in other organs.

With the exception of the diapasons, as mentioned above, flutes blend well with most other stops for solo use. They can often be employed with excellent effect combined with imitative orchestral reeds, and full combinational advantage may be taken of the several pitches, both of flutes and orchestral reeds. Generally speaking, the flute will take the higher pitch better, say, for example, clarinet 8 ft and flute 4 ft, but the reverse is often quite happy, e.g. lieblich bourdon 16 ft and clarinet 8 ft, or for special effects, cor anglais 16 ft, clarinet 8 ft, and flute 4 ft can sometimes be employed. Again, the 2 ft piccolo (if not too loud) may quite well be added to, say, orchestral oboe 8 ft, or other light imitative reeds. The piccolo will blend occasionally with string tone with quite good results, but this is not always so. To be effective, it must be dead in tune.

There are also flute-toned stops which give two distinct pitches per note, the ground tone and its twelfth above in about equal proportion. These are the quintaton family,

16, 8, and 4 ft pitch, and the quintadena, generally 8 or 4 ft pitch. The note C would give in addition the G an octave and a half above.

The quintaton 16 ft makes an admirable double, of good blending quality, if not added to the chorus too soon, but, apart from ensemble use, both these stops are most valuable colouring agents, and impart a delightful piquancy to solo combinations, particularly when used with imitative orchestral reeds.

CHAPTER VIII

MUTATION STOPS

STOPS which give a note other than that of the actual key struck, or its octaves above or below, come within the generic term "mutation stops." The purpose of these stops is twofold in character. Firstly, they help to bind together the ensemble of the foundation stops (8 ft), sub-foundation stops (or doubles 16 ft), and the stops giving higher octaves. The manual quint $5\frac{1}{3}$ ft has been referred to already. This function of binding together the various pitches of the ensemble is by no means unimportant and none too well understood or appreciated, but the second of the twofold offices of mutations is perhaps even less realized by both builders and players alike. This is the function of affording distinct tonal alteration or colouring to a great variety of combinations.

It is only in recent years that the study of mutation stops has been revived in England, although the rich effect of mutation stops of the baroque period has never been entirely lost on the Continent (see Chapter XX). Obviously these registers not giving the pitch of the note played will produce a recognizable musical "interval" between themselves and those stops which give either the note played, or its octaves. For example, the twelfth $2\frac{2}{3}$ ft on the great organ, if drawn with the principal 4 ft, will give the interval of a fifth, or if drawn with the diapason 8 ft, the interval of a twelfth, from which indeed it receives its name. Similarly, the tierce (or seventeenth) $1\frac{3}{5}$ ft would give the interval of a major third, if drawn with a 2 ft stop, and so on. This fact leads to a helpful general rule in the use of mutations, viz. never combine mutation stops in such a manner that the interval can readily be detected. If, in solo use, consecutive intervals can be heard, there is either too much mutation, or too little foundation or octave pitch in the combination. When such a combination is employed in chords, or in several moving parts, the result is still more unsatisfactory, for the mutational intervals are tuned "dead," and these will set up a horrid dissonance with the intervals of the tempered scale.

The mutations, then, must be so combined with other stops that a definite tone colour emerges without unduly revealing the harmonic intervals.

As all organs differ from each other, and are so much affected by their surroundings and environment, it is impossible to lay down hard and fast rules for this type of combination. Again, it is a case of individual experiment upon the organ concerned, and its effect in the building. The following suggestions, however, have proved very effective and highly satisfactory on a number of instruments: flutes 8 and 4 ft + nazard $2\frac{2}{3}$ ft; flutes, and other quiet 8 and 4 ft stops + tierce $1\frac{3}{5}$ ft; the same + nazard and tierce with or without 2 ft stop.

For ensemble purposes. For choral playing in chords: The full soft combination of the choir + nazard, tierce, or both. Occasionally the addition of a soft 16 ft and septime $1\frac{1}{7}$ ft to the above may prove satisfactory.

For solo playing. The addition of one or more mutation stops to the solo registers of the organ is most valuable, if not overdone. I have frequently found the following combinations to be entirely delightful: clarinet, cor anglais (16 or 8) or orchestral oboe + nazard, tierce or both; clarinet, cor anglais, or orchestral oboe + quintaton 16 ft. This stop (as mentioned before) gives the twelfth in addition to the ground tone, but the imitative reeds generally absorb this harmonic to a large extent, and the result is an interesting modification of the tone quality.

On some organs keen string tone like the viole d'orchestre

will blend with the mutation stops in much the same way as suggested above for the wood-wind group, and I have found occasionally that the violes célestes could be included in the combination quite successfully.

To the above combinations flutes 8 and/or 4 ft may sometimes be added with advantage, nor must the brightening qualities of the piccolo 2 ft (or 1 ft where available) be overlooked. These may be used with the orchestral reeds quite happily on some organs, with or without the use of the mutation stops proper. The tremulant can be added (in discreet doses) to all the above combinations of mutation stops, but this must not be overdone.

The septime $1\frac{1}{7}$ ft which gives the interval of a flat 21st (not quite B♭ against the C held) needs treating with a little care, in order to avoid dissonance. Introduced together with the right amount of foundation tone it imparts a quaint reediness to the tone, with or without the use of other mutations at the same time. It can be used to colour the more powerful violes. This produces a quasi-orchestral oboe of rather quaint tonality, but the separate mutational interval must not be recognizable.

The use of piccolo, nazard, and tierce, together with a lieblich gedeckt 8 ft, sometimes gives a remarkable synthetic clarinet. Very occasionally bell or glockenspiel effects are required. These can often be produced from flutes and mutations. One of the best I obtained was on the solo organ in Cavaillé-Coll's noble instrument (now destroyed) in the Albert Hall, Sheffield. It consisted of bourdon 16 ft, flute harmonique 8 ft, and tierce $1\frac{3}{5}$ ft.

There are many instruments in England in which the only mutation stop is the great organ twelfth $2\frac{2}{3}$ ft. In some instances, unfortunately, the twelfth rank is permanently tied to the fifteenth 2 ft. Thus the use of the twelfth as an independent stop is impossible. Where the twelfth draws individually it is well worth trial to see at what point in the build-up of the ensemble it produces colour and clarity. There are times when this is only made apparent when using a small number of stops in the ensemble. Again, some twelfths blend admirably with the flutes, giving a somewhat piquant tonality, equally useful for solo effects, or in music containing two or three parts only.

CHAPTER IX

MIXTURES (COMPOUND STOPS)

COMPOUND stops consisting of two or more ranks of various harmonic intervals have raised no little controversy from time to time. To scale, voice, and regulate them successfully is one of the severest tests of artistic organ building. There are some who consider that the function of mixture stops is merely to corroborate or enhance the natural harmonics of both flue work and reeds, thus brightening the tone. In this way the gap between the two classes of tone can be bridged. This, of course, is one of the useful offices performed by mixtures, which should help to bind together both flues and reeds into a true cohesive ensemble. But mixtures do much more than this. Happily, during the present century they have received increasing attention, and something of the glory of the colourful effect of the old continental compound stops has been re-captured. Some of the old "cornet" mixtures can be used as delightful solo stops, alone or in combination. Alas, it is true occasionally, even yet, that mixtures merely scream at one, but I have found that many mixtures can be used (as they should) to top the flue ensemble without reeds. On large organs at least two mixtures each on great and swell are desirable, and these should give both colour and point to their ensembles.

One has however to play the organ as one finds it, different indeed though it may be from one's ideal. Even so, a few experiments are well worth trying, for I have discovered from time to time that mixtures which seemed to give but little promise have produced interesting compound tonalities when combined with various carefully selected registers. These resulted in combinations quite worthy of inclusion in our list of useful effects, especially when heard at a distance, and invaluable when playing certain types of organ music.

In using a mixture in solo combinations, when it was not originally designed for that purpose, there is, of course, the snag of breaks. Breaks are those points in a mixture where one or more ranks *break* back into pipes of lower pitch, owing to the upper ranks having ascended to the shortest pipes of practical or effective usage. Generally there are two main breaks in the compass of five octaves, with a third near the upper extremity, but this is not a hard and fast rule. In certain continental "cymbale" mixtures, the whole set of ranks breaks back every octave! If therefore your solo melodic line takes you above or below a break, a different tonality will result. This, however, ought not to happen in public, as experiment should reveal it at once.

Organists and students are well advised to hear, as well as to play upon instruments containing a number of artistic compound stops, e.g. the Schulze Organ, in Doncaster Parish Church, which has three mixtures each on great and swell. Once again good chorus or mixture work added at the correct moment will give the much desired clarity to the ensemble.

In English organs the corroborative or ensemble mixtures are normally composed of diapason pipes, in order to enhance the natural harmonics of this, the most important family of organ stops. There are, however, a number of instances, (e.g. at Ely and Liverpool Cathedrals, and the Royal Albert Hall, London, amongst others), of string mixtures, named "cornet de violes." These enhance the harmonics of the string-toned stops.

On the Continent the constituent ranks of compound stops often incline towards flute tone, and indeed definite flute ranks, both open and stopped, are sometimes included in "cornet" stops. Tapered gemshorn pipes are also used occasionally. The most elaborate mixture played by the writer is the "Grossmixtur," 12 to 16 ranks, in the church of St. Lawrence, Nuremberg.

In America the study and re-development of colouristic mixtures is receiving considerable attention.

CHAPTER X

PEDAL STOPS

THE poverty of the pedal department in a vast number of English organs is much to be deplored. This is scarcely surprising in view of the very late introduction of the pedal clavier into England, long after highly-developed pedal schemes had appeared on the Continent. Even to-day there are many two-manual organs with only one pedal stop, an indifferent bourdon 16 ft. In such cases one is almost compelled to couple one or both manuals to the pedals in order to obtain definition. No variety of tone is possible, but relief from the wearisome drone is obtainable by silence, or by using pedal couplers only. In the accompanying of hymns and psalms occasional rest is most desirable, even with a large and varied pedal organ, still more so with a limited pedal scheme. (In the orchestra, the double basses do not always play at the same time as the violoncellos.) Large numbers of moderate-sized two-manual instruments possess only a bourdon 16 ft, and bass flute 8 ft, the latter obtained by extension, and therefore, only the bourdon played an octave higher, with twelve small pipes added for the upper octave. This 8 ft section is invaluable for solo use when voiced and regulated by an artist, but in some commercial instruments the lack of finish in this rank of pipes suggests the hand of an apprentice. Again, the 8 ft stop alone will give a certain amount of point to the bass, when coupled, in playing accompaniments. These remarks also apply to other 8 ft flue stops whether obtained by "extension" or not.

On larger pedal organs the over-use of the weighty open wood 16 ft must be avoided. It should be remembered that clarity of the bass parts is of very great importance. Open

PLATE III. WALKER CONSOLE, DONCASTER PARISH CHURCH,
BUILT TO THE DESIGN OF THE AUTHOR
(By courtesy of J. W. Walker & Sons Ltd., Ruislip, Middlesex

PLATE IV. ROTHWELL CONSOLE (ROTHWELL PATENT STOP
CONTROL), ST. GEORGE'S CHAPEL ROYAL, WINDSOR CASTLE
(*By courtesy of Frederick Rothwell & Sons (Harrow), Ltd.*)

16 ft stops, such as the violone, contre bass, and contra viole, with their 8 ft companions, whether made of metal or wood, add greatly to the appreciation of the true contour of the bass part. One or two builders prefer to include a metal 16 ft open diapason for this reason. In later years the contra dulciana 16 ft has been more frequently provided, even in some very small organs. This stop (like the contra gamba and contra salicional) is much richer in harmonics than the ubiquitous bourdon, and consequently more interesting and less wearisome. Either of these stops can be added to the bourdon with advantage.

In many instruments such registers are borrowed from manual doubles, but some are individual pedal stops, to the immense gain of that department. There is a superb example of an independent contra gamba 16 ft on the pedal at York Minster.

It was a joy to hear the late Sir Edward Bairstow use this stop as the bass to varied tone colours on the manuals. The effect is beautifully clear and penetrating, yet quite soft and unobtrusive. The greater the variety in tone and power of the 8 ft and 4 ft stops on the pedal organ, the less the need of manual-to-pedal coupling. This results in a more individual and interesting bass part to the music, and in much greater clarity, if and when the pedal part soars above any of the parts played on the manuals.

Only those who have experienced it can appreciate the value of a completely independent pedal organ such as one finds in large continental organs, where the whole tonal structure, including flue work of 32, 16, 8, 4, and 2 ft, together with mutations of various pitches, mixtures, and reeds 32, 16, 8, and 4 ft, are all independent stops. Schulze, however, saw no harm in pedal extensions as exemplified at Doncaster and elsewhere. True, these fine schemes lack some of our charming soft derivations from manual doubles, and the dignity imparted by our English open wood 16 ft;

but the grandeur and definition afforded by a really complete pedal department made up of independent stops is very striking.

Of recent years the diaphone (introduced and probably invented by Robert Hope-Jones) has been improved to a remarkable degree by the John Compton Co., and their diaphonic contra basses, 32 ft and 16 ft, have given us registers of great dignity, promptitude, and drive.

Stops of 4 ft, though on the increase, are still rare in English pedal organs. Apart from their obvious use, where demanded in some of Bach's *Choral Preludes* and other works, they greatly enrich and clarify the ensemble of the pedal organ. They are of immense value in polyphonic music.

Only a few of our pedal organs contain mutation ranks and mixtures. These, of course, are generally based on 16 ft pitch as their foundation, and are in consequence an octave lower than their manual counterparts. A good pedal mixture imparts considerable grip and incisiveness to an appropriate pedal combination, and the mutations, where available, give colour and effectiveness which are very valuable.

There is one pedal mutation which requires a little care in use. This is the quint $10\frac{2}{3}$ ft. If a separate rank, and therefore tuned "dead," it will give a 32 ft undertone acoustically, when combined with 16 ft registers in the lower octave. This tends to thicken the bass considerably. It may, however, enhance a real 32 ft effect, but in the upper reaches (especially when composed of open pipes) the interval of a fifth between the 16 ft and $10\frac{2}{3}$ ft stops is sometimes distinctly audible until a reed is added. Further, I have occasionally heard only too clearly the discrepancy between the "dead" fifth of the quint in the upper octave, and the "tempered" fifth of a chord held on the manuals. I have also noticed similar unpleasant effects in the upper reaches of the pedal clavier where a manual quintaton 16 ft has been borrowed as a soft pedal stop.

32 FT STOPS AND PEDAL REEDS

Undoubtedly one of the noblest effects of the organ is that of real 32 ft tone, whether obtained from full-length open pipes (wood or metal), the 32 ft stopped contra bourdon, the remarkable polyphone bass of the Compton organ, or from the fine diaphonic 32 ft stops of that firm.

A good 32 ft flue stop in a building of reasonable acoustic properties can be used in the lower octave with even the softest manual stops. It will also add greatly to the majesty of the louder combinations, including the full organ itself. It should not generally be used without the addition of one or more 16 ft stops of appropriate power. It may however be used alone for a moment at the end of a quiet movement, or of an improvization while the choristers are entering before service. In this case, the pedal couplers should not be employed. The 32 ft flue stops should not be over-used. Their lower notes are not very effective in rapid playing; their true grandeur is best appreciated in sustained passages.

It is impossible to generalize on the use of 32 ft reeds. They vary greatly in power and in quality. Environment also plays no small part in their effectiveness. Of course any 32 ft reed will add to the splendour of the full organ, but for other uses each such stop has to be considered individually. Some 32 ft reeds can be used effectively by themselves as a pedal bass for the full swell. Others are too vague in pitch to be used without the addition of 16 ft reeds. Very occasionally a 32 ft reed is effective when employed with full great flue-work without reeds. Modern examples are generally fairly prompt in speech; nevertheless the best results are obtained when the 32 ft reed is employed in slow-moving passages, long-sustained pedal points, and final powerful cadences. With rare exceptions (as indicated above) the 32 ft reed is added to the rest of the pedal organ, including reeds. Once more, experiment is desirable in order to obtain the best results.

In this country there is a vast number of organs possessing no pedal reeds whatever, and a good many with but one powerful 16 ft reed, and perhaps an 8 ft stop extended from it. The two together are intended for use in full-organ passages, but either may be effectively used with full swell coupled to the great diapason chorus (minus great reeds), and even more effectively with the great to mixtures uncoupled. With full pedal flues, used in this way, the 16 ft reed will mark out the bass when accompanying a large congregation; to a lesser degree the 8 ft reed will do the same. The latter, if of good quality, is also useful as a pedal solo stop. The 4 ft reed, where this exists, can also be used for solo purposes. In large instruments, however, the solo tuba coupled in 8 ft or 4 ft pitch will give this effect with probably superior tone quality. Occasionally this stop is made playable independently on the pedal organ, which is a great convenience, and leaves the solo keyboard free for other effects. Apart from its solo use, as in some Bach *Choral Preludes* and other works, the 4 ft reed gives valuable definition to the full pedal.

On the Continent a 2 ft pedal reed, named choral bass, is not infrequently found in larger instruments. This again adds point and clarity to full passages, as well as being invaluable for solo use in certain works of the *Choral Prelude* type. This 2 ft reed is not as a rule very powerful or very fiery, its quality being something like that of a small trumpet.

In large pedal schemes an independent fagotto (or bassoon) 16 ft is sometimes included, and this may well form a connecting link in building up the power of the pedal organ by degrees. Such stops too, like borrowed 16 ft reeds from the manuals, add a crispness to combinations of medium strength. Borrowed 16 ft orchestral reeds such as the contra clarinet, cor anglais or contra bassoon, are delightful when used occasionally for quasi-orchestral basses. They generally blend well with the quieter flue stops, and at times can be used as basses for the wood-wind group for special effects.

CHAPTER XI

COUPLERS

SINCE Victorian days the number of couplers provided in organs generally has steadily increased. This is largely due to the fact that many builders, both in America and in England, prefer to make independent intermanual octave and sub octave couplers, rather than have their octave and sub octave couplers *acting through* the intermanual and manual-to-pedal couplers. In the smaller two-manual organs, this means an increase of two or three additional couplers.

For example: the normal two-manual organ, where the octaves *act through* the unison, would have the following couplers, viz. swell to great, swell octave, swell sub octave, great to pedal, swell to pedal. Now suppose that the swell to great, swell octave and sub octave couplers be drawn. If middle C be depressed on the great, the C above (octave) and the C below (sub octave) would sound on the swell in addition to the unison. This is called "the octaves acting (or reading) through the intermanual couplers." In like manner, where the action is pneumatic or electric, the manual octave couplers may read through the manual-to-pedal couplers. In the old mechanical or pneumatic-lever action, where the intermanual or manual-to-pedal couplers actually move the keys of the manual coupled, any coupler drawn on that manual automatically functioned, or read through.

Now if it be desired to make all these coupler effects independent, then in the case of our hypothetical two-manual organ, four additional couplers would be required, namely, swell to great octave, swell to great sub octave, swell to pedal octave, and swell to pedal sub octave. The last named is rarely found, and is quite unnecessary. Where the octave couplers read through, the provision of a "unison off" on manuals possessing their own octave couplers enables these octave couplers to be played through the intermanual or manual-to-pedal couplers. Thus it produces the effects of intermanual, or manual-to-pedal octave couplers; but in so doing, the unison is removed from the keyboard concerned, and its use is considerably restricted thereby. The "unison off," though not strictly a coupler, is considered as such, and is grouped with the octave couplers for the sake of convenience.

Having seen that, in order to give complete independence of coupling, three or four additional couplers are required, even for a small two-manual organ, it necessarily follows that, for a large five-manual instrument, an enormous number of couplers will be required if similar independence is to be achieved. Some organ builders in England, and most of them in America, label their couplers according to pitch, i.e. sub octave 16, unison 8, octave 4. This is a very convenient arrangement. Thus, the full complement of couplers for a five-manual organ can readily be set out and apprehended as follows—

Swell to great	. 16, 8, 4	Choir to pedal	. .	8, 4
Choir to great	. 16, 8, 4	Solo to pedal .	. .	8, 4
Solo to great	. 16, 8, 4	*Echo to pedal	. .	8, 4
*Echo to great	. 16, 8, 4	Swell (on self)	.	16, 8, 4
Swell to choir	. 16, 8, 4	Choir (on self)	.	16, 8, 4
Solo to choir .	. 16, 8, 4	Solo (on self) .	.	16, 8, 4
*Echo to choir	. 16, 8, 4	*Echo (on self)	.	16, 8, 4
Great to solo .	. 16, 8, 4	Solo to swell .	.	16, 8, 4
Great to pedal	. 8	*Echo to swell	.	16, 8, 4
Swell to pedal	. 8, 4			

Total 51 Couplers

On a four-manual organ, the couplers marked * would, of course, be omitted, thus reducing the number of couplers by 14, and couplers great to solo 16, 8, 4, are only found occasionally. Even so, for the normal four-manual organ we have the considerable number of 34 couplers. On the other hand,

where floating bombarde and/or positive divisions are provided, these sections sometimes have their own independent
octave couplers; also independent intermanual and pedal,
unison and octave couplers, thereby making a considerable
further increase in the total number of couplers. "Floating"
divisions are those sections of a large organ which have no
independent keyboard of their own, but are made available
on one or more keyboards by means of drawstops, stop keys,
tablets or other forms of switch (e.g. bombarde on choir,
bombarde on solo, positive on choir, positive on great,
orchestral on solo, etc.). Floating echo organs are to be
found in many organs in America.

There are instances of echo organs being played from four-
manual consoles, e.g. Westminster Abbey, Leeds Parish
Church, and others. In such cases rocking tablets (or other
forms of switches) connect the echo organ to various keyboards at will; and either the echo organ has its own individual octave couplers, or is affected by any octave couplers
drawn upon the manual to which it is for the moment
connected.

Now to what use can all this vast array of couplers be put?

Like all other good things, couplers can be (and some often
are) abused. Many organists, alas, rarely allow the fine clear
fresh tone of the great organ ensemble and its lesser combinations to be heard, without at least some part of the swell
organ being coupled. The over-use of the swell to great is
most unfortunate, for one should frequently hear the great
organ in all its open clearness, especially in contrapuntal
music. Indeed in some cases, so rarely is the great keyboard
used uncoupled, that the swell to great knob would seem to
be redundant! I have heard the late Sir Edward Bairstow
speak very strongly on this subject.

There is a tendency in some quarters to make too much
use of octave couplers. Now it must be borne in mind that
they are limited in compass. The octave coupler usually runs

into nothing in the top octave. Its effective compass is forty-nine notes only, and if the music soars into the top octave, the upper notes have no corresponding octave above, and therefore the melody is destroyed. If the music is chordal, then the lower notes of the chord (below the top octave) are doubled in the highest octave, and sound above the melodic line. To overcome this difficulty most organ builders in America carry the compass an octave higher than the keyboard concerned (i.e. to 73 notes) to complete the compass of the octave coupler. This is a rather expensive but highly effective and artistic procedure, which has rarely been done in this country up to the time of writing. (A notable instance is the swell organ in St. James Church, Whitehaven.)

Similarly the sub octave coupler has an effective use from tenor C only, this note, of course, sounding the lowest note CC. If, therefore, with the sub octave drawn, a chord be played the bass note of which is in the lowest octave, the bass note alone will not be doubled in the octave below. Not only does this mean a weaker bass, but if the next note of the chord is in the tenor octave, this will be sounded by the sub octave coupler in the lowest octave, and may readily be below the true bass of the chord! For example: Take the common chord of G.

There being no lower G for the sub octave to sound, the bass of the complete chord becomes D, and thus a chord of $\frac{5}{3}$ is perverted into one of $\frac{6}{4}$! Further, the G first line is already sounding, so it is not reinforced by the sub octave coupler from G fourth space. Thus the true proportions of the chord are lost, as well as the true bass, G, the very root of the chord being largely ineffective. A little thought will show that, if octave and sub octave couplers are employed in playing close contrapuntal music, the presence of weak notes here and there may ruin the melodic contour of the inner parts and of the treble line, if the music ascends sufficiently high, whilst the melodic line of the bass may be hopelessly distorted.

The moral is obvious, viz. avoid the use of octave and sub octave couplers in contrapuntal or polyphonic music, otherwise confusion will result. Be sure, when using these couplers, that the music lies within their compass at both extremities. Organ playing in general, and registration in particular, brings the player up against a peculiar snag which needs to be carefully guarded against and avoided. This is, that the organist, aided by the sight of his music copy, may hear in his mind the intended sounds, rather than the real sounds he is producing as heard by his audience. To this may be added distortion and confusion caused by the reverberation of buildings and the relative position of the listeners.

It is here that the player must make sure that octave coupling does not destroy the clarity of the music. The music must come first, always, before any splendour of effect or colouring. Many full swells will stand the octave coupler well, if the above rules are adhered to, whether played from the swell keyboard, or coupled to the great or choir. Likewise the sub octave if the music is placed high up on the keyboard. All these effects must stand or fall by their own merit on the individual instrument concerned. Some organs will admit the use of swell to great octave without the unison, even with full swell, or the swell to great sub octave without unison, with a limited amount of swell stops drawn, generally including upper work.

Frequently a well-balanced great will stand the use of choir to great unison and/or sub octave, with full choir drawn.

This is especially the case if this department is equipped with mutations or mixture and a splashy little trompette to top the ensemble. A similar use with part of both great and choir is often good.

String-toned stops readily admit the use of octave couplers, both in solo and harmony, especially if the chords of the latter are well spaced, and the occasional cutting out of the unison by "unison off" produces quite an ethereal effect. Owing to the profusion of natural harmonics in string-toned pipes, the loss of the unison is not so obvious as might be expected.

Dulcianas and salicionals take octaves well, and the occasional massing of these with string tone by the coupling of swell and solo to choir in unison, octave, and sub octave, or by various combinations of these couplers, will produce superb effects in some organs. Suitable music is, of course, assumed.

The grand lower notes of the pedal 32 ft flue may sometimes be used with these combinations, with noble effect.

Octave and sub octave couplers can be used with various solo stops. Piquant effects too can sometimes be obtained by using sub and octave couplers with appropriate solo stops or combinations together with the "unison off."

Other uses of couplers have already been mentioned in dealing with speaking stops. One further use should be mentioned, that is the coupling together of the quieter stops of most or all keyboards. A comparatively soft and rich ensemble sometimes results which can be obtained in no other way. Of course this ties up the keyboards, and thereby limits the use of this effect. Further, the effect is not good on some organs, or in some buildings. It is never suitable for contrapuntal music, but only for quietly moving chordal music. On a large organ a considerable variety of charming effects may be obtained this way, and a skilful use of the several swell pedals admits of dissolving the combinations drawn upon each keyboard, or bringing them into greater prominence, at will. Octave and sub octave couplers, within the limits of their compass, may be included in these combinations.

Finally, what about the use of *all* couplers, 16, 8, 4 with full organ? This can rarely, if ever, be artistic. Possibly, when accompanying several thousands of people singing lustily in a very large church, or civic hall, it may almost be a necessity. I have done this myself on occasion (when no choir or chorus was present) to keep the huge singing mass under control, but though necessary, it was not a desirable effect from the artistic point of view.

CHAPTER XII

THE TREMULANT

THE tremulant is, of course, an accessory, not a speaking stop. Its function is to excite periodic repercussions in the wind supply of the department of the organ to which it is attached, e.g. swell, choir, solo, or echo organs. In the legitimate organ it is rarely made to affect those stops on heavy wind, or the great or pedal organs. On the cinema instrument, tremulants are supplied to all ranks, and are generally rather violent in action.

Tremulants are fondly imagined by some to imitate the vibrato of the human voice, or of the violin family, but the tremulant being a mechanical device, the pulsation is regular, and so the illusion will in no wise hold good. To overcome this in some measure, one or two builders (notably Willis and Harrison) have occasionally given us tremulants with variable speeds.

The stops which bear the addition of the tremulant best have already been mentioned *en passant*. Its occasional use with small ensembles of flutes, strings, and possibly an enclosed small diapason, with or without a soft reed, is sometimes valuable. Some swell or choir diapasons will take the tremulant for solo use quite well, as, for instance, the open diapason on the swell at York Minster.

Once again the over-use of violent tremulants in the cinema gives one pause. I fear that the worst examples deserve to be renamed ditherants. Therefore, beware of the over-use of a rather mechanical device, which is invaluable if used artistically and with discretion.

CHAPTER XIII

THE VOX HUMANA

No organ register has been more abused than the vox humana. In fact, this abuse has actually led to the rejection of the stop in a number of rebuilds.

Truth to tell, the quality of the vox humana varies greatly in different instruments, and some of our greatest organ builders have produced rather sorry specimens, probably due to their own lack of approval of the type. Again, the appalling abuse in cinema instruments (in some instances containing quite good examples of the stop) has led to its abhorrence on the part of the purist. If it is voiced on French lines, after the manner of the great master Aristide Cavaillé-Coll, the stop can be very effective for occasional use. Normally the tremulant is drawn with the vox humana, which may be played in solo or in harmony.

It can also be employed in solo without tremulant in certain organs, but not always.

The ear is the authority on the matter, and each stop has to stand (or fall) by its own merits, or the lack of them; for sometimes the tremulant covers a multitude of voicing irregularities.

Used with discrimination the vox humana is a valuable timbre creator, if in good tune. It may be added to imitative orchestral reeds, flutes of various pitches, string-toned stops, or combinations of all these types. I have met with examples where an enclosed diapason used with vox humana and tremulant has produced a very tolerable broad solo 'cello effect.

The late Edwin H. Lemare was an adept at making these combinations. He would build up from strings *ppp* to fairly loud effects, step by step, and by very subtle use of the vox humana and swell pedals, keep up the feeling of ever-increasing quasi-orchestral string tone.

Again, a really good vox humana, used without tremulant, will sometimes act as a capital substitute for a baroque reed in suitable music, and to it may well be added mutation and light 8 ft, 4 ft, and 2 ft stops. This, of course, needs trial by experiment on the organ concerned. When successful it proves a really valuable addition to organ tone-colouring. Such effects, however, should not be over-used.

CHAPTER XIV

DEVICES TO AID REGISTRATION

SINCE the invention of composition or combination pedals, generally attributed to Bishop, many contrivances, sometimes elaborate in design and mechanism, have been devised to assist the player in the control of the stops, either singly or in groups.

There are still a considerable number of organs with only two or three composition pedals acting upon great and swell stops respectively. Frequently the composition pedals for the great affect the pedal registers also.

Whatever combinations these pedals give were fixed when the organ was built, and the player is expected to accept them, and to modify the results they give by direct hand registration.

Not infrequently these original combinations of stops are far from happy, especially that selected for the full-swell composition pedal, and in a somewhat lesser degree that given to the full great. In the vast majority of cases each stop is moved "on" or "off" by a fan which engages with a small wooden block screwed at a convenient point on the stop rod concerned. To the practical organ builder it is not at all a difficult matter to alter these blocks. Consequently, when the player has (by careful experiment) decided which group of registers constitutes his best and clearest full swell and full great (from the listener's point of view), the help of the organ builder should be obtained.

The small expense involved will be amply justified by the results. The other composition pedals may need similar correction.

There is occasionally a possible snag with regard to the full-great composition pedal, especially in older organs, owing to the fact that sometimes they are single acting, i.e. they can only add stops, without withdrawing any. In such an instance the composition pedal almost invariably puts on *all* the stops in the department, including dulciana, gamba, and all flutes. The addition of these often destroys the clarity of the diapason chorus, and also shows up any out-of-tuneness or "robbing" there may be.

Now a single-acting composition pedal comprises no mechanism to withdraw these stops. Consequently it is best to remove the blocks of those registers which are undesirable, so that, at any rate, this composition pedal will not put them "on."

The above remarks refer to fixed mechanical composition pedals, but they also apply to tubular-pneumatic combination pistons or pedals. Many of these are simply a pneumatically operated version of the mechanical type.

In some varieties, however, they are actuated by individual pneumatic motors, a pair for each stop, one for the "on" position, and one for the "off" position. When this is the case it is often quite easy to alter the tubes concerned, in order to obtain the desired combinations.

Should the action be electric, the adjustment of the wiring presents no serious obstacle.

ADJUSTABLE COMBINATIONS

The idea of making all combination pistons or pedals readily adjustable by the organist, without recourse to the use of tools, is rapidly becoming more and more a standard practice in organs of reasonable size.

Apart from one or two special forms of "adjustable" combination mechanism, peculiar to their makers, there are two chief methods of adjustment, namely the "switchboard" type and the "capture" system, where either a master-setter piston is used to adjust all combination movements, or individual "setter" pistons are provided for each adjustable piston.

In the first type a switchboard is fitted on or near the console. Sometimes there are two, one for the stops of each jamb, right and left respectively. On these switchboards are movable pneumatic blocks, or electric switches, one for each register affected by each piston. Thus, for twelve registers and five pistons the total number of blocks or switches would be sixty. Each switch has three positions, "on," "neutral," "off." Thus the player can arrange for any particular combination on any piston, and also, by using the neutral position, leave any stop unaffected by any piston at will. The earliest application of this system on a large scale in this country was accomplished by Henry Willis when he rebuilt the organ in Hereford Cathedral in 1893. This was operated by tiny draw knobs (a set for each piston) placed above the ordinary stops of the department concerned. These gave "on," "neutral" and "off" positions; and the settings were actually visible to the player. This wonderful piece of mechanism continued to function for forty years, till the organ was again re-constructed by the present firm in 1933, when it was replaced by the "capture" system. Unfortunately it was allowed to be removed from the Cathedral to the works, and it perished in the London fire blitz in 1940.

The advantage afforded by the neutral position is but little understood. Here is a simple example of one of its many possible uses. Suppose we have a small choir organ with only four pistons, and we set on piston (1) dulciana only; on piston (2) salicional and gedeckt; on number (3) full choir; and on (4) clarinet alone. Having done this, we wish we had another piston on which we could set the 4 ft flute in addition to the combination on piston (2). Now if on piston (2) we set the 4 ft flute switch to neutral, we can easily obtain this effect. By pressing the full-choir piston, thus putting "on" the 4 ft flute, and then pressing piston (2) the desired result will be obtained, for the flute being set neutral will remain "on." Suppose, however, that instead you want piston (2) without the 4 ft flute. All that is necessary is to press piston (1) followed by piston (2). Piston (1) will remove the 4 ft flute, and this stop being set neutral will remain "off" when piston (2) is pressed. Thus again, the desired combination is obtained. It is important when both changes are being made in this manner that the hands are for the brief moment clear of the keys, otherwise the double effect will be heard.

Beautifully made examples of pneumatic switchboards by Henry Willis can still be seen in perfect working order at St. Bees Priory Church, Cumberland (1899), and elsewhere.

In recent times Messrs. Harrison & Harrison of Durham have employed very small knobs grouped in neat glass cases placed near the consoles of several of their large organs having electro-pneumatic action. The principle of "on," "neutral," "off," however, is similar to that used by Willis at Hereford in 1893.

Electrical combination switchboards giving the three positions are very compact, and are sometimes placed in drawers or cupboards at the console, or even behind the music desk.

In the "capture" system combinations are adjusted either by means of small setter pistons placed above the stops of the department concerned, or by one master-setter piston for all combinations. In the former case, having drawn the stops required, simply press the setter piston bearing the same number as the one upon which it is desired to set this combination. Instantly, the selection of stops drawn for the department concerned will be set on the piston bearing that number, and will remain so until reset. Obviously any combination in use, even during actual playing, can be set, if a hand can be spared for a moment to touch the individual setter piston.

The master setter is generally placed well away from the ordinary pistons, often to the extreme left of the choir key slip. Should this piston be pressed alone nothing whatever happens. To set any combination, the master setter must first be pressed in and kept so, while the piston upon which it is desired to set the combination is also pressed. Both setter and piston are then released. Whatever stops are drawn in the department concerned (i.e. great, swell, choir, pedal, etc.) will automatically be set on the particular piston so pressed. As an example: Suppose we desire to set full swell on swell piston No. 7. First draw the selection of stops giving the best and clearest full-swell effect. Next, press the master-setter piston and retain it while pressing swell piston No. 7. Instead of No. 7 piston giving the combination which was previously set thereon, it will accept the full-swell combination selected, and, on release of the setter, will retain this combination until reset.

In like manner, any piston for any department operated whilst the master setter is pressed will accept and set whatever combination of stops is drawn for that department at the time, and will give that combination whenever pressed, until it is reset.

GENERAL PISTONS

General pistons usually affect every register in the entire organ. They were first introduced by Willis at St. George's Hall, Liverpool, in 1855, and were removed in 1898. They were re-introduced by the present firm in 1931 and made adjustable on the "capture" system.

In the modern organ they can control the speaking stops of every department, manual and pedal, all couplers, and all tremulants. On some instruments only one or two generals are provided, each giving instantly a predetermined combination most frequently required, such as great diapasons with full swell coupled, suitable pedal stops and appropriate pedal couplers. Another might give a solo stop on one manual, and a suitable accompaniment on another, together with the required amount of pedal, and suitable couplers. On many large modern instruments, however, *adjustable* general pistons are provided, the combination for the entire instrument being set as described above, either at switchboards, or by master setter. Adjustable generals are most useful in making complete and rapid stop changes of the entire organ, as required in some modern organ compositions, or in transcriptions from orchestral scores. A further use, which the writer has on occasion found invaluable, is to set on some of the general pistons the complete registration for the opening of the more important items in a recital programme. Thus, at the conclusion of one piece, a single touch on the appropriate general piston will prepare the organ instantly and correctly for the next piece.

As a rule, pistons adjusted by a master setter afford no neutral position for the registers they control. The Compton Organ Co. are contemplating its inclusion in future design, which will be a considerable asset.

COMBINATION COUPLERS

A useful device is the coupling together of certain departmental combination mechanisms. The most usual coupler in this class is great and pedal combinations coupled. When this coupler is in use any great piston will operate the internal mechanism of its appropriate pedal piston (or composition pedal) thus providing a suitable pedal bass to the combination given by the great piston. In like manner any pedal piston (or composition pedal) will operate the mechanism of its corresponding great piston. There are two other varieties of this coupler: (1) great pistons to pedal combinations, and (2) pedal combinations to great pistons. When the former is in use, the great pistons operate the stops of the great organ only, but the pedal combinations operate both pedal and great organ stops; whereas if the latter is in use, the pedal combinations only affect the pedal registers, but the great pistons affect both great and pedal stops.

The coupler pedal to swell pistons, when drawn, causes each swell piston to give a suitable pedal in addition to its swell combination. Similarly the pedal to choir pistons provide an appropriate pedal for the choir piston combinations. This combination coupler, however, is rarely found. Less rare, happily, is the coupler pedal and accompaniment to solo pistons. When this coupler is functioning it causes the solo pistons not only to provide a suitable pedal bass and coupler, but also an appropriate accompaniment on another manual for the solo stop (or stops) given by the solo piston concerned.

Most of the above combination couplers were used by Willis at Lincoln Cathedral in 1898, and St. Bees Priory in 1899. The two couplers, great pistons to combination pedals and pedal to great pistons were first united into one movement by Messrs. Harrison & Harrison in their famous organ at St. Nicholas, Whitehaven, in 1904.

In more recent times it has become the practice of several firms to provide second-touch pedal combinations for the majority of their manual pistons. A further pressure on the piston, against a strong spring, gives a suitable pedal for the manual combination given by the first touch. Other forms of piston coupling exist, but they are not often found and need not be discussed here.

CANCELS

At first sight, the idea of having a piston or pedal to take "off" all registers belonging to a particular department, or even of the entire organ, seems somewhat strange. In large instruments separate cancel pistons are generally provided for each manual department, for pedal stops, and one isolated general cancel for all registers. Sometimes also a separate cancel piston takes off all couplers, and another affects the octave couplers only, leaving all unison couplers free. A little thought will show that, with a large number of stops in each department, it is a great convenience, simply by pressing a piston, to take "off" all the registers of any department. One can then draw one or more stops for a special effect. Such a change can be made much more rapidly than if one had to push in a number of stops (possibly widely separated) by hand, before drawing the few stops required for the special effect.

The general cancel is a useful, and not very expensive luxury. Some great players recommend its use at the end of every piece, or section of the church service. In this way a clean slate, as it were, is presented, and a fresh outlook is encouraged before beginning to play again.

The second-touch cancel (Messrs. J. W. Walker's patent) is a very effective and useful device. If any drawstop is pulled forward slightly, beyond the normal draw, and against a strong spring, all the other stops of the department which may be out are automatically withdrawn. In like manner, the further pressing down of any stop key, against a strong spring, causes all the others of the department concerned, which may be "on," to assume the "off" position. This is very helpful indeed when one or two stops only are required, and a considerable number are functioning. It is a standard practice with Messrs. Walker, and Compton. The latter use the patent by arrangement with Messrs. Walker.

Some builders provide cancel bars which extend over the rear portion of all or most of the stop keys of each department. On these being depressed, any stop keys of that department which may be "on" return to the "off" position. In the Rushworth and Dreaper type of cancel, short *black* stop keys project over the rear ends of the stop keys proper. When any one of these black keys is depressed, any stop keys which may be "on" return to the "off" position, and in addition the stop key below it is put "on." The black cancel keys are omitted from the few stops not likely to be used alone.

REVERSIBLE PISTONS (OR PEDALS)

As the name implies, these pistons reverse the position of

any coupler or speaking stop they control, i.e. if "on," the pressing of the piston will put that register "off," and vice versa. For this reason the American builders call them "on-or-offs."

For many years the vast majority of organs possessed but one reversible, that for the great to pedal coupler only. Nowadays reversibles are often provided for all unison couplers. The convenience this affords in a large modern organ having perhaps thirty or more couplers is considerable.

The more important, such as swell to great, great to pedal, solo to pedal, and especially solo to great, are often duplicated by reversible toe pistons or pedals. The latter enable the player to couple and uncouple the solo tuba whilst holding chords on the great with both hands, as occasionally demanded when interpreting certain French works on the English organ (e.g. Guilmant's 1st *Sonata*, first movement), or at other times when both hands are engaged.

Occasionally reversible pistons are provided for single speaking stops, such as the tuba, pedal 32 ft flue, 32 ft reed, 16 ft reed, etc. These are well worth while, particularly the reversible for the pedal 16 ft reed, as it provides for pedal solo, and return to pedal bass at will, which is very useful in playing Bach.

At St. Bees Priory there are no reversibles for the pedal couplers. Under each manual there is a piston on the left of the others which draws the manual-to-pedal coupler, and withdraws the other two. This accomplishes in one movement what would require two or possibly three movements had each coupler been provided with a separate reversible piston.

This arrangement was unique until Messrs. Compton reintroduced it in more recent times. This admirable device is not suitable, however, in those instances where the intermanual and octave couplers are unaffected by the pedal couplers, because the lower notes of the department coupled to the manual and/or the effect of the octave couplers (as the case may be) would be lost. For example: If the swell to great be drawn, when the great piston is pressed, it would withdraw the swell to pedal, and, as in this form of independent coupler action, the great to pedal affects the great organ only, the lower notes of the swell would be absent. In such instances separate reversibles are most desirable.

DOUBLES OFF

A device which will remove all doubles (i.e. manual 16 ft, and pedal 32 ft stops) without interfering with the actual registers is a useful accessory. It is sometimes desirable to clarify the ensemble in use for a period in contrapuntal or polyphonic passages, or during a fugal entry. As the stop knobs or stop keys of the doubles are not moved by doubles off, any such stops if drawn when it is operated will sound again when it is put "off." This contrivance is generally actuated by a small horizontal rocking tablet placed on one of the key slips, or it may be controlled by a reversible piston, or better by two pistons labelled "on" and "off" respectively. The one pressed remains in, pushing the other out, and indicates which is in use. Occasionally a small spot-light indicator glows when the doubles off is functioning. It is most necessary that its action shall not be completely "blind."

THE GENERAL CRESCENDO PEDAL

Theoretically this apparatus builds up the stops in correct sequence from *ppp* to *fff*. It may do so in actual fact, but as it is operated by a balanced pedal exactly like those used for controlling the swell shutters, the natural limitations of our ankle movement prevents so fine an adjustment from being fully effective. Its chief use is to retain a certain amount of power (mostly from *forte* to *fortissimo*) on both manuals and pedal, whilst fresh combinations are being prepared under cover of it, to be brought into play when the general crescendo is put "off." It can also be employed for *sforzando* effects, as demonstrated with good results by the late Dr. Alfred Hollins. As a rule, but not invariably, an indicator is provided to show the amount of power given by the crescendo pedal. Frequently this indicator is mechanical in action, sometimes tubular-pneumatic, and in some instances electric, in which case it is frequently luminous. The luminous indicator is the most effective, for it also acts as a warning to the player that the pedal is in operation. Except in the case of luminous stop control (described in Part One, Chapter II) the indication shows the amount of power only, and not the actual stops in use. It is, therefore, one form of blind registration which is dealt with later in Chapter XIX. One or two firms have produced adjustable general crescendo pedals, which are a great advantage.

CHAPTER XV

DOUBLE TOUCH

LITTLE has been written about the possibilities of double
(or second) touch in relation to organ registration.
Doubtless this is due to its comparative rarity in the
ordinary organ. Probably introduced by Robert Hope-Jones
round about 1887, it consists of a shallow second touch, the keys
being pressed deeper, beyond the first or normal touch. It is made
against springs sufficiently strong to prevent the player from
pressing accidentally through the first into the second touch.

It is applied to both manual and pedal claviers. Hope-
Jones used the second touch chiefly for operating important
couplers, such as swell to great, solo to great, solo to pedal,
etc. Later he made a number of speaking stops similarly
available individually, such as the tuba, clarinet, and other
solo registers. The pedal diaphone was also included. In
England the growth of appreciation of double (or second)
touch as a means of amplifying registration has been very
slow indeed, except in the cinema instrument. It became
rather more popular in America, due largely to the fact that
electric action was generally accepted as the standard organ
mechanism. The Americans were some twenty years in
advance of us in the matter of electric action.

The value of double touch was soon recognized in the
cinema, where it was used successfully for percussive effects.
Unfortunately the music played was all too often poor, and
even debased in character. Such players as Quentin Maclean
and others, however, employed the device with very great
artistry in more serious music.

The Compton Organ Co. were quick to realize the possibilities of second touch, and introduced it into a number of

their important organs. There were signs of its increasing favour a little before the second Great War. Two notable examples come to mind: a solo to pedal, 2nd touch, was included by the Willis firm in their rebuild of the Birmingham Town Hall organ in 1933, and a solo to great, 2nd touch, appeared in the Harrison & Harrison rebuild of the organ in King's College, Cambridge, in 1934.

Double touch may be employed in various ways. The following suggestions, based on simple chords, are not to be looked upon as music, but are merely given as examples of the use of double touch.

In order that the reader may perceive quite clearly the results obtained by double touch I have set out the actual effect of the 2nd touch as a separate stave. This would not, of course, appear in the ordinary printed copy.

EXAMPLE I

Accents and sforzando effects are readily available on 2nd touch couplers. In example 1 a very strong accent is obtained quite easily on the first beat of each of the two bars shown. It is only necessary to draw solo to great 2nd touch, with the

solo tuba, and to press down hard with the right hand only
on the accented beats. The accent may be cut off sharply, or
retained to the full beat as shown.

EXAMPLE 2

Example 2 shows an accented beat of less power. The
swell to great 2nd touch coupler is drawn, and the full swell.
The full swell is added to the first beat of each bar, by pressing
through into 2nd touch with the right hand only.

In example 3 the solo to pedal, 2nd touch, and 16 ft bassoon
are drawn. The pedal passage is given point on the strong
and weaker rhythmic accents, by pressing through into 2nd
touch on the accented notes *only*. The amount of accent on
these notes would be regulated by the solo swell pedal before
the passage was commenced.

Double touch may be used with fine effect in *pedale doppio*
passages such as the one illustrated in example 4. Here the
upper pedal part is brought out on the solo clarinet with
comparative ease.

Pedal passages such as those found in Hollins's *Triumphal
March*, where the tuba has to be coupled to the pedals

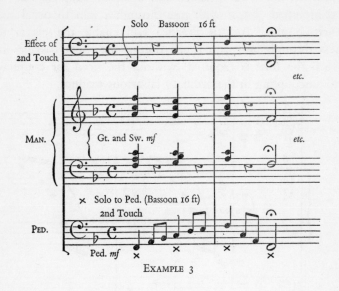

EXAMPLE 3

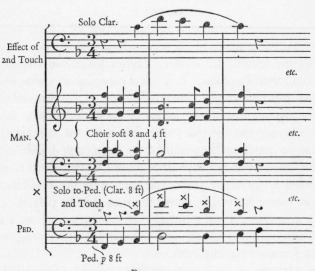

EXAMPLE 4

repeatedly for short periods, and again uncoupled, can be accomplished almost with ease through a solo to pedal 2nd touch coupler. A little practice will enable the player to press through into 2nd touch during the short passages in which the tuba is required, without the need for coupling and uncoupling in the ordinary laborious manner.

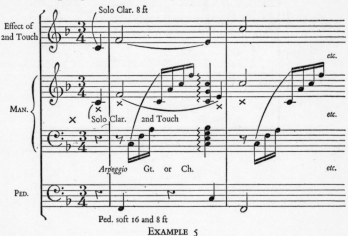

EXAMPLE 5

The playing of sustained or continuous solo parts by 2nd touch on the manuals requires considerable skill, but it is well worth the trouble to acquire. Hymn tunes and chants can be used for this purpose. Any vocal part, soprano, alto, tenor, or bass can be brought into prominence, as a contrasted solo, or merely emphasized, by means of the second touch. In the first instance the desired single solo stop (or combination) would be drawn on the manual to be coupled in double touch. In the second instance such stops would be employed as were intended to combine with, and augment, the combination on the parent keyboard, where the tune is to be played.

Occasionally an inner melody may be sustained on a solo stop through 2nd touch, and surrounded by arpeggios or other forms of accompaniment.

In example 5 we have a simple melody surrounded by

arpeggios. If the only 2nd touch coupler is the solo to great,
and it is desired that the arpeggios be played on swell or choir,
it is necessary to couple the swell or choir to the great, without
drawing any stops on the latter.

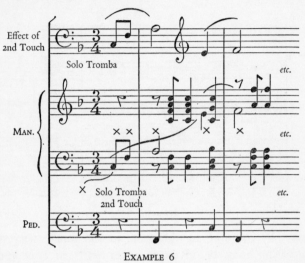

EXAMPLE 6

In example 6 the melody is divided between both hands,
and the accompaniment consists of chords above and below it.
In both examples the notes to be pressed through into 2nd
touch are marked X.

Example 7 is really an exercise. It consists of a tuba fanfare
and a Tierce de Picardie climax, played through 2nd touch
from the great and pedal, while holding big chords over a
tonic pedal throughout the entire passage. It is not as easy
as it looks, but in its mastery the student will be amply
rewarded. For practice purposes, a soft great and a distinctive
stop on the solo organ are all that is necessary. I venture to
hope that the simple illustrations of double-touch effects here
given will help the reader to realize some of the possibilities
afforded by the device, and that they will suggest many other
ways in which it can be artistically employed.

When once proficiency in playing on a keyboard equipped with 2nd touch is obtained, more subtle uses become available, quite apart from the strongly-contrasted effects of solo and accompaniment, accents, or climaxes mentioned above. For

EXAMPLE 7

instance, by coupling suitable stops in 2nd touch, very slight accentuation may be given to inner parts in contrapuntal music, in order that these may be heard more clearly by the listener in the building, away from the organ. Fugal entries in the inner parts may sometimes be so treated, where strong contrast would be undesirable, even if it were possible by playing them on another manual.

Again, phrases may be slightly emphasized by either hand with complete artistry, or the pedal part enriched for short passages through double-touch pedal couplers. By a judicious selection of the registers available on second touch, it is sometimes possible to suggest real phrasing in a manner quite unobtainable without this valuable mechanism.

PLATE V: RUTT CONSOLE (LUMINOUS STOP KEYS), CHURCH
OF ST. MARTIN-IN-THE-FIELDS, LONDON
(By courtesy of Robert Spurden Rutt, Leyton, London)

PLATE VI. TYPICAL FRENCH CONSOLE BY CAVAILLÉ-COLL
(*By courtesy of A. Senior, Esq., Sheffield*)

CHAPTER XVI

SUSTAINERS

ANOTHER device which is very slowly being recognized as a means of augmenting the possibilities of registration is the sustainer. This is really a logical development of the *prolongement* familiar to us in certain harmoniums of French manufacture. The mechanism can be applied to both manual and pedal claviers, and is brought into play by draw knobs, stop keys, luminous touches, or pistons. Sometimes the toe piston functions rather like the sustaining pedal of the pianoforte; consequently, while it is depressed, any note or chord played on the manual concerned is sustained until the toe be lifted from the piston, when it is released. Others have reversible mechanism by which the sustainer is controlled. The action may be mechanical, tubular-pneumatic, or electric. The last is the most usual form. It is not unduly expensive to install when a new instrument is being built, or when the action of an existing organ is being electrified. I have come across one or two instances where, with the sustainer "on," depressing a note would automatically release any other note or chord held by the sustainer, whilst the note depressed would itself be sustained. Occasionally this form is applied to the lower octave only of the pedals. By such means long bass notes widely spaced can be sustained and released by an occasional quick movement of the left foot. This leaves both feet more or less free for elaborate pedal work in the upper octaves. Mr. Herbert F. Ellingford is an adept at this form of virtuoso pedalling. In the last reconstruction of the famous St. George's Hall Organ, Liverpool, a pedal divide was introduced. This enabled the lower octave to sound the pedal stops (by sustainer if desired) while the upper reaches were free to be used independently through the pedal couplers. Mr. Ernest M. Skinner and other builders in America have included the pedal divide in their large instruments. The demand for the use of sustainers by composers of organ music is indeed slight. Such pieces as Dubois's *Marche des rois Mages* and similar works come to mind, but a little weight or a match-stick will do all that is required in this case. None the less the device can be used occasionally with great effect. Even in Bach there are times when certain notes, such as inverted pedal points, may be sustained with excellent results, leaving the hands free for more perfect phrasing of the remaining parts. Again, many subtle artistic touches may be achieved by this device during accompaniment. To record even a few of these and to give the necessary musical examples would occupy many pages. Here are some suggestions which may stimulate thought: single notes held on any solo stop, leaving both hands free for full accompanimental work above, below, or around them; and intervals such as major or minor thirds, or other chords similarly treated. If not overdone, the tuba, sustained in single notes, octaves, or chords offers attractive possibilities in this direction. Occasionally big chords on the great full to mixtures may be held by sustainer, and fanfare or other passages played on the tuba.

Sustainers, however, come into their own most appropriately in real improvisation. Here the great artist has full scope to use his imagination. Never shall I forget a six tone-colour improvisation played by M. Marcel Dupré on the organ in his studio at Meudon, near Paris. For this he employed sustainers on two of the keyboards for the greater part of his marvellous performance. *En passant* it may be mentioned that the action of the sustainers on this organ was visible, as the actual keys remained depressed until released.

On another occasion the organist prepared large chromatic chords on the sustainers, with no stops out. These chords were brought into play when desired, by drawing soft string-toned stops, while wonderful decorative work was played all around them on other manuals with quiet registers of contrasted tone. During improvisation on these lines the artistic effects obtainable by the use of sustainers are almost endless. Would that such great art were more developed in this country!

CHAPTER XVII

ORGAN PERCUSSIONS

Percussion stops of any kind are very exceptional in the ordinary British organ. In America, however, two musical percussions, the so-called harp and chimes are the rule, even in instruments of modest dimensions. Cinema instruments, of course, abound in percussions, musical, rhythmic, and special effects such as fire bells, etc.

What is called the harp is in reality a beautiful set of mellow-toned metal bars. These are placed over carefully tuned resonators. They are struck by electro-pneumatic hammers. The tone is luscious, soft and pervading. It combines well with the quieter registers of the organ, especially flutes, and generally with strings. I have come across several examples of American manufacture, where keen violes combined with harp (or a similar stop called chrysoglott) and played staccato in arpeggio passages, suggested the presence of a real orchestral harp. The viole imparted the suggestion of the peculiar attack of the plucked string, and the evanescent tone of the genuine harp was simulated by the fading vibrations of the metal bars. Obviously then, as the organ harp can be used much in the manner of the orchestral instrument, its name is not inappropriate.

The chimes are a beautiful set of tubular bells, accurately tuned. Often their use in organ music is directed by American composers, and where chimes exist the wishes of the composer should be respected. Even to-day such stops are rare in British organs. For many years there were only two notable examples: one in the celestial organ at Westminster Abbey, and the other in the echo organ at Norwich Cathedral. These were resonating gongs. I experimented with both of them. Each

stop was excellent in its own way, and combined well with
the flue stops of its own department. At Christmas time the
late Sir Frederick Bridge used these gongs at Westminster
Abbey with great artistry when improvising between the
carols. One of his favourite combinations was gongs together with the slowly undulating flauto unda maris. The
sound of the gongs faded away, leaving the unda maris
sounding. To hear this effect descending from the triforium,
about 300 ft from the console (and above the tomb of
Handel), on such occasions, while the last rays of a winter's
sun illumined the stained glass, was a pure joy. Possibly
sentimental, yes, but sentiment in the correct place, and at the
right time.

The slightest over-use of percussions, however charming,
becomes cloying and nauseating. Restraint is the secret
of their effective and artistic use. Never employ them,
unless some real musical advantage is gained thereby.
Resonating metal bars and chimes have been introduced
into several important new and rebuilt instruments in
more recent times, and in one or two instances the actual
bars of the orchestral glockenspiel have been incorporated.
They can occasionally be used effectively in organ music
of the scherzo type; but again, artistic restraint is demanded.
Not more than one item in a normal recital programme
should be so treated, and even then only if it is really
appropriate.

Very occasionally other percussions of a non-melodic type,
such as drums, triangles, cymbals, etc., are included in the
instrument of our concert halls. These can only be used as
they would be in the orchestra, for playing transcriptions,
and for popular entertainments. They have as yet no place
in the genuine organ repertoire.

Percussions have been brought to a very high degree of
perfection, both in tone-quality and effect, and also in mechanism. Most of the few appalling examples (more like

children's toys than musical instruments) which existed some
years ago, have happily gone for ever. The German builders
have re-introduced the ancient Cymbalstern, which might well
be called a baroque percussion stop. It consists of a visible
golden star of some size placed high up on the organ case.
This star rotates when in use, and jingles small tuned bells.
Some organs possess several of these Cymbalsterne, the bells
being tuned to the more usual keys (G, D, A, C). Surprisingly,
perhaps, they can be used with real musical effect.

Should any reader wish to pursue the subject further, a
comprehensive list of percussions and effects, together with
diagrams of their mechanism and control, will be found in
The Cinema and Theatre Organ by the present writer.

CHAPTER XVIII

CONTINENTAL STOP CONTROL AND REGISTRATION

I.—French

THE purpose of this and the following chapter is to give the organ student some idea of the kind of instrument for which continental composers have written, and still write. It is intended also to show something of the type of stop control, and to give an indication of the tonal features of their instruments. The tone quality and method of stop control adopted by the French and German organ builders has had a considerable influence on the organ music of these countries. This applies more to French than to German organ compositions, although in the latter case the influence is quite evident.

The organ student is well advised to study these instruments at first hand, when at all possible. The translation into English of registration indications in copies of French and German organ music can be very misleading to the player who has only a knowledge of English organs. It is hoped that the following remarks will prove helpful.

THE FRENCH ORGAN

To consider first the tonal aspect. It is important to realize that the big heavy open diapason of many English instruments is entirely absent from the French organ. The montres 16 and 8 ft which correspond to them are comparatively quiet, but beautifully clear. On them is built up a rich ensemble through the prestant 4 ft with ample mutation ranks leading up to fourniture III–V ranks. Sometimes there is also a powerful cymbale IV ranks which repeats every octave. This latter has to be used with considerable discretion. Its purpose is to bind the entire flue ensemble to the powerful blaze of the French chorus reeds 16, 8, 4 ft.

The flutes and gambe are all transparently clear, and blend well with the montres. In larger organs several quiet mutation ranks assist in the formation of rich ensembles of medium power. Some of the cornet or similar mixtures afford most valuable colouring. This matter of the blending power of French flue work is of prime importance.

As will be seen later, much French registration consists almost entirely of coupling or uncoupling ensembles of different power and quality.

French string tone is not of the keen Hope-Jones type, neither is it of the quiet Willis variety. The gambe et voix célestes is moderately keen but very transparent in quality. Moving inner parts when played on it can easily be distinguished, in a manner all too rare in English instruments.

The French imitative stops, basson et hautbois and clarinette are each beautiful, and can be employed as in English organs. They possess, however, a certain characteristic tinge or flavour very difficult to describe. The voix humaine and tremblant (or tremolo) is sometimes called for in the works of certain French organ composers. Tonally, this mock pathetic register reaches its most perfect form in the best French examples. Whatever we may think of the abuse of this stop in England, particularly in the cinema, we should not lightly ignore the composer's direction for its use in French organ music. It is, as it were, the colour the artist had in mind for that portion of his picture; and we have a moral obligation to present, as far as possible, the composer's work as he conceived it.

The chorus reeds, bombarde 16, trompette 8, and clairon 4 ft, are powerful and very free in tone. They sometimes speak horizontally direct into the church or hall. These trompettes en chamade, as they are called, produce a sheer blaze of sound. When suitably placed on the solo, or other convenient manual, they can be used as we use the tuba, but their tone quality is quite different, being essentially "trompette."

The pedal department in large organs is often a complete and independent ensemble, from 32 ft flue to 4 ft and mutations, plus very powerful free-toned reeds comprising 32, 16, 8, and 4 ft pitches. A pedal bombarde 16 ft is often found in comparatively small instruments. Borrowing and extension are rare, and the valuable weighty and dignified open wood 16 ft, so familiar to us in English organs, is absent. There are but few 16 ft flue stops, and it is for this reason that we find occasionally, in the works of Widor and others, the indication bourdon 16 ft on one of the manuals, to be played through the appropriate tirasse, or pedal coupler. The pedal 4 ft flue stop is often a corno dolce or flute of great beauty, designed mainly for solo use, and quite different in quality from any other flute in the organ. This fact explains such instances as are to be found in Vierne's *Symphonie* III, where difficult chords are given to the pedals with 4 ft alone, even when one hand or both are free to play such chords on the manuals.

THE FRENCH VENTIL SYSTEM

The plate of a typical large French console (facing p. 87) will repay close study. This console (no longer in existence, alas) was almost identical with the one which Guilmant had in view when he wrote much of his organ music. To-day the standard type of French console is still the same. Only very slowly are Anglo-American, or quasi-German consoles appearing in France. Note the terraced drawstops, and the long reaches involved. Fussy stop-changing simply cannot be done. In the noble and immense instruments in Notre Dame Cathedral, St. Sulpice, and the Sacré Cœur in Paris, these terraces are made in quadrant form. Even so, the reach to the extreme right and left is considerable. Notice also the iron hitch-down pedals. Before I had this photograph taken I hitched down one or two of them in order that they might show more clearly.

From left to right these pedals were: effet d'orage (storm effect) which is the raised crescent-shaped pedal on the extreme left. When pressed down, it operated the action of the five bottom notes of the pedal organ from CCC to EEE, in succession, retaining them while depressed, and releasing them in succession as the pedal was raised—it did not hitch down. Whatever pedal stops were in use at the time sounded exactly as they would have done if the pedal keys themselves had been depressed. Apparently the idea was to obtain a variety of drum-like effects, rather than (as its name suggests) forming the master ingredient of Storm Fantasias of the Lemmens type.

It was an unholy terror if operated by accident.

Continuing towards the right were four hitch-down tirasse pedals for grand orgue (gt), positif (choir), récit (sw) and solo (pedal couplers). Note that the grand orgue pedal has had an ugly wooden extension added. Then came the five anches pedals (reed and upperwork ventils) for pédale, grand orgue, positif, récit, and solo respectively. Next pédales à bascule (balanced pedals) for positif and récit boxes. Still continuing to the right, under the heading "copula" were grand orgue main ventil, octave grave grand orgue (gt sub), positif à grand orgue, récit à grand orgue, solo à grand orgue (choir, swell and solo to great respectively), récit à positif (swell to choir). The grand orgue main ventil was not strictly a ventil in the true sense of the term, but a coupler for connecting or disconnecting the action of this department to or from its keyboard. If this pedal were not hitched down no stop (reed or flue) could sound on the grand orgue, but any other key-board coupled to it could be played from it. On the right of the "copula" pedals were the two "tremolo," récit and positif, and lastly a huge lever swell for the solo, excepting the unenclosed horizontal chamade, tuba magna 16, trompette 8, and clairon 4 ft. Only a small portion of the solo lever swell pedal can be seen in the photograph.

It will be realized that all couplers, including tirasse (pedal couplers) were operated by pedal only. There were no composition pedals or pistons.

The stops of the pédale occupied the two lower terraces right and left, those of grand orgue (bottom manual) the next terraces above. The stops of the positif (second manual) were on terraces three and four on the left, while those for the récit (third manual) occupied the corresponding terraces on the right. The two upper tiers were for the stops of the solo (fourth manual).

The registres de combinaison or ventil knobs next claim our attention. These were all placed on their respective terraces nearest the keyboards. Where the stops were divided between both sides, e.g. pédale, grand orgue, and solo, two ventil knobs right and left were provided, one only being allotted to each of the undivided groups positif and récit. Now the ventil knobs merely admit or shut off the wind from the drawstop mechanism of the department concerned. If these ventil knobs are not drawn, the drawstops are "dead," and as the internal pneumatic-lever mechanism is balanced, the stops remain *in situ*, "on" or "off," in exactly the position as they were when the ventil knobs were put in. It must be understood that these registres de combinaison do not interfere with the wind supply to the actual windchests.

In order to "prepare" the organ, therefore, *all* the ventil knobs must first be drawn to admit wind to the drawstop action. Next, the drawstops themselves must be drawn for our first combination. Now if the ventil knob (or both if there are two) is, or are, put in, the particular combination is locked, and a second one can be "prepared" on the knobs. This second combination can be brought "on" at will by drawing the ventil knobs of the departments concerned.

Where there are two knobs, either will bring the new combination "on," but both must be closed during preparation of a further combination (otherwise the wind will not be cut off from the mechanism, and the stops will function).

The Anches Ventils. The hitching down of these pedals admits wind to the reed soundboards of the department concerned. Generally, with the exception of the pédale and chamade, the reed chests also bear most of the mutations and mixtures. The stops governed by the anches ventil of each section are lettered in red. Thus, any of these stops lettered in red (even though drawn) can never sound unless their anches ventil is opened, and any such stop as may be drawn (subject, of course, to the control of the ventil knob, which may be holding the actual knobs drawn for a second combination) can be put "on" or "off" by opening or closing the anches ventil by its pedal. For example: supposing certain anches, say mutation or mixture stops, were locked by the particular ventil knob, and reeds added in the "prepared" second combination, the anches ventil would only add or subtract the mutations or mixtures, although the reed stops would also be drawn (prepared). The English translation of the word "anches" is generally given as reeds. This may be misleading. That this is not necessarily the case has, I hope, been shown above. The player must consider the actual context of the music before making his decision as to the registration of such passages on an English organ. If, of course, the indication be *Anches fff*, then no doubt exists. Reeds *and* Flues are intended.

The octave grave is mechanical in action, and affects the grand orgue pneumatic-lever machine. It therefore operates through all couplers associated with the grand orgue. This means in English terms that the great sub-octave coupler can be used from the great keyboard, through the swell to great, choir to great, and solo to great couplers, as individual sub-octave couplers on those manuals, the great being silenced by closing the grand orgue main ventil (without interfering with the other knobs or ventils). This is one of the important uses of this so-called ventil, which is really regarded as a grand orgue-to-pneumatic machine coupler, which in fact it is. Other uses of the device occur in the French method of building up collective ensembles of moderate power by coupling the various keyboards to the grand orgue. A little thought will show that this makes possible the union of, say, solo and récit, or solo and positif, by coupling these to the grand orgue, and disconnecting the grand orgue temporarily by means of the so-called main ventil. This does not interfere with the stops of that department, which can be added when required by merely hitching down the appropriate pedal.

I have dealt with the French console at some length, because unless the English organist has some idea of the tonal differences and control of the French organ, he will experience real difficulty in registering French organ music. Most of the larger and very many smaller organs in France (and also to some extent in Belgium) are to-day controlled as above described.

If the reader has grasped the main points of what has been written above he will recognize clearly the influence the French organ has had upon French organ music, sometimes to its detriment. Numerous examples could be quoted. A glaring instance is Guilmant's *Marche Funèbre et Chant Séraphique*. Look at that musically barren bridge passage between the *Marche* and the *Chant Séraphique*, and read carefully the registration instructions *in French*. There are vast numbers of less obvious, and not necessarily unmusical instances in the works of most French organ composers. Many large movements in the works of César Franck, Widor, Vierne, Guilmant, and others are entirely registered by the hitch-down pedals, that is, by coupling or uncoupling small or large ensembles; and by opening and closing the anches ventils which control mutations, mixtures, and/or reeds. In our endeavour to adapt

French organ music to the English instrument, we need to consider the context of the music itself, and not be led away by mistranslations of the French registration.

Just a word of warning about the hautbois et trompette, directed to be used at times by César Franck for solo effects, in movements of a rather contemplative nature. On the organ in the Church of Sainte Clothilde, Paris, he had a small trompette of great refinement—almost an orchestral oboe. It was this stop he had in mind, not the fiery trompette proper —an important point. Even an English swell trumpet would be too big. Franck was not the only composer to specify the use of stops peculiar to his own organ.

Another rather misleading indication is the word "Fonds," or "Fonds de 16. 8. 4. p," etc. As this word is translated into English as "foundation stops" with or without pitch indications, the big English diapason with heavy double not unnaturally comes to mind. This of course was never intended by the composer. More often than not, a comparatively quiet ensemble is required. The true character of the music itself is the surest guide. I have heard organists obey the injunction "foundation stops" literally, and not only draw the big diapason, but also all other 8 ft and 16 ft flue stops, to the destruction of the composer's real intention.

It will be understood, of course, that the above remarks refer to the main or "grand orgue" proper, not to the petit orgue de chœur, which is often quite a tiny instrument, with little or no pedal organ. The purpose of the latter is the accompaniment of the choir only, and it is sometimes helped out with stringed instruments, especially in the bass.

CHAPTER XIX

CONTINENTAL STOP CONTROL AND REGISTRATION

II—*Germany and other countries*

TONALLY the German organ is somewhat harder in the quality of its flue work than the French instrument, though often possessing sparkling and brilliant mutation and mixture work. The chorus reeds are not so free and fiery, but a marked cohesion of both flue and reed ensembles is frequently apparent. As in the French organ the typical big English diapasons are lacking, and one rarely finds a solo reed of tuba quality or power. Some modern examples include excellent copies of baroque stops (see next chapter).

The well-recognized contrasts in character of the English great, swell, choir, and solo organs, or of the grand orgue, récit, positif, and bombarde (or solo) of the French organ, do not appear to be nearly so standardized in the various manual departments of the German instrument. Nor again is the difference in the power so great between the Hauptwerk, Brustwerk, or Oberwerk of the older organs, as between the great, swell, and choir departments of the English instrument.

In the modern German organs the manual departments are very frequently numbered Man 1; Man 2; Man 3, etc., and do not bear the distinctive titles of Hauptwerk, Brustwerk, or Oberwerk. Sometimes the word Schweller or Schwellwerk is added, to indicate that the department is enclosed, e.g. Man 2 (Schwellwerk).

As with older instruments, the difference in power between the ensembles of the several manual divisions is not so great as in the English organ. Thus, in the larger organs, and in some of medium size, there exists what practically amounts to *two* great organ ensembles, similar in power, but of different quality. This is a great asset when playing some of the works of Bach, Reger, and other composers.

Something similar is to be found in one or two of the largest French organs, which possess a bombarde division in addition to the grand orgue. In England the provision of two contrasted great organs is all too rare. The fine schemes recently carried out at Norwich Cathedral and Brompton Parish Church are recent examples, and there were two great organs at Manchester Cathedral from 1910 up to the time the cathedral was destroyed by enemy action. Messrs. Compton have included a bombarde section in several of their larger organs.

The Fernorgel (fern = far or distant) or Fernwerk of the German organ is a long-distance echo organ. This is often very complete, with a fully-developed tonal structure, and independent Fern pedal organ.

GERMAN STOP CONTROL

The tilting-tablet form of stop key has found great favour among German organ builders, and is used almost exclusively. In the smaller organs these are placed over the keyboards, below the music desk; and in the larger instruments, they also occupy jambs, or terraces, sometimes in quadrant form.

Stop-moving combination pedals or pistons are rare. Mechanical aids for controlling the registers are never very numerous, even in the largest instruments. Three or four pistons for each manual department, and a like number for the pedal, with possibly three or four general pistons controlling the entire organ, usually suffice.

There is in addition of course, the customary Walze, or Rollschweller. The pistons register by remaining "in" when pressed, and are released by an "Auslöser" piston—one such

PLATE VII. STEINMEYER CONSOLE, PASSAU CATHEDRAL, GERMANY

(By courtesy of Hans Steinmeyer)

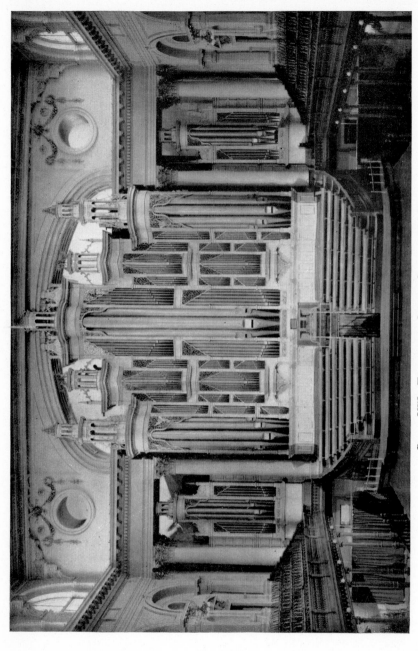

PLATE VIII. TOWN-HALL ORGAN, SYDNEY, N.S.W.

Built by Hill & Sons, London, this is the only organ in the world that contains
a complete full-length 64 feet reed stop.

being provided for each group—or the piston itself is released, by being eased upward somewhat. In this case a slight downward pressure when it is pressed home causes the piston to slip into a notch, and thus to be retained in the "on" position until eased upward. Generally the pistons have a much greater range of movement than we are accustomed to in England.

There are two main forms of piston control, namely the "Freie Kombination," and what we call the "blind" form of combination. The illustration of the immense console for the organ in Passau Cathedral, Bavaria (228 speaking stops) clearly shows the former.

Above each tilting tablet will be observed four tiny knobs. These (over a thousand in number) are for the "Freie Kombination." They are in fact miniature stop knobs. They can be drawn at will, and a combination prepared and set on them. Each row is numbered 1, 2, 3, or 4 for the division concerned. These little stops remain inoperative until their respective piston (corresponding to their row) is pressed "in," and retained. Instantly the tilting tablets are put out of action, and the row of tiny knobs bearing the number 1, 2, 3, or 4 comes into operation, and remains so until the piston is released as described above.

These are "*Freie* Kombination" in a double sense. In addition to their use in preparing a "freie," or as we say, an *adjustable* combination in advance, the tiny knobs are *free* while operative, and can be used exactly like the larger stop knobs of the English organ, and the registration changed at will. It will thus be seen that five combinations can be prepared in advance, one on the tilting tablets, and four on the little knobs (called "Züge") of the Freie Kombinationen. Sometimes miniature lever stop keys are employed for the Freie Kombinationen instead of, or in addition to, the tiny knobs or Züge.

As at Passau, all the thumb pistons are frequently placed on the keyslip of the lowest keyboard. This allows of the manuals being somewhat closer together than in English organs.

The Walze, Rollschweller, or crescendo roller, is a much more important accessory on German organs than the English general crescendo pedal. It can readily be seen in the photograph, and consists of a rubber-covered roller which can be rotated backwards or forwards by the foot. Not being limited in movement like the balanced pedal, it can actually be made to build up the power of the organ stop by stop. Frequently it does this, and a comprehensive indicator shows almost exactly which stops the roller is controlling. A great variety of these indicators exist. In the photograph that for the Walze and the pedal moderator (a narrow roller of slightly greater diameter on the right of the Walze) can be seen above the treble end of the fifth manual. The Pedalmoderator is a crescendo roller for the pedal stops only. In some organs these indicators are much larger, and even give individual stop names. As at Passau, there is often a device for putting the Walze "on" or "off." This may be operated by hitch-down pedal, or it may be controlled by pistons—Walze ab, and Walze an. It is thus possible to prepare a desired amount of organ tone in advance, and to bring it into play at will by the contrivance mentioned above. I have witnessed German organists make very good use of this device.

German pedal organs generally are more adequate than ours, and not infrequently possess a complete individual ensemble. The use of pedal couplers, therefore, is less necessary, and accessories to control them are not so frequent. In large organs, however, sundry devices are found for special effects such as: Tuttipedal for each manual, Generaltutti for the entire organ, Pianopedal Man 1, 2, 3, Zungen ab (= reeds off), Zungenchor or reed chorus, and others. These are generally operated by pedals or pistons, which are sometimes provided also to control groups of couplers. Occasionally, the German equivalent of our doubles off is found.

BLIND COMBINATIONS

The second kind of combination action often found in German instruments is the "blind" type. In this form the pistons are numbered 1, 2, 3, and 4 respectively, and generally remain "in" when pressed. They are released either by the "Auslöser" piston, or by an upward movement to disengage them from a notch, as in the Freie Kombination type. There are, however, no little knobs or "Züge." When pressed, and while the piston remains "in," a fixed combination (the combination arranged when the organ was last in the hands of the builder) takes the place of the combination shown on the stop keys, and these latter become "dead." Thus, a new combination can be set if required, while the piston is in operation. On release, whatever combination is shown on the stop keys comes into play, and the latter becomes operative again. Often the fact that the piston is "in" forms the only indication that it is functioning. Consequently the ears of the player alone can guide him as to what stops he is actually using. A visit to the interior of the instrument, if the player is sufficiently skilled in organ mechanics, will confirm this. Hence, there being no *visual* registration, this form of combination is called "blind." True, in many examples the pistons are indicated by the appearance of tickets behind windows placed under the music desk. These windows are blank unless and until any particular piston is pressed, when its ticket numbered 1, 2, 3, or 4 appears at its window. If the player does not know what is the effect given by any particular piston, he is still in the dark. Occasionally more precise information as to power—*pp*, *p*, *f*, or *ff*—is printed on the tickets. When the piston is released the ticket disappears. The idea is rather reminiscent of a cash register.

In some very recent examples the indication is luminous. I came across instances where small spot-lights warned the organist that piston number so-and-so was "on." The registration, however, was still "blind" concerning what stops were actually in use.

In both forms of combination action the pressing of one piston will as a rule automatically release any other piston within its group.

With the exception of the late firm of Brindley and Foster of Sheffield (who exploited "blind" combination action very fully) this form of registration has found little favour with English organ builders or players.

In many German organ consoles the entire equipment of stop keys is numbered consecutively. Some organists keep a record of the combinations to be prepared for the more important items of their repertoire, using these numbers instead of stop names. I have seen privileged pupils "prepare" the organ ready for their master's performance, using manuscript combination record books containing numbers only.

OTHER CONTINENTAL COUNTRIES

So far as I have been able to discover, by personal experience and inquiry, no Continental countries besides France and Germany have produced a national, or distinctive type of organ, or of stop control.

Apart from the superb old masterpieces of international fame (which may Heaven preserve!) to be found in most countries in Europe, the German type seems the more usual. I found one firm in Holland which favoured the Hope-Jones lever type of stop key, together with stop-moving control. Again in Italy at Milan, I tried a large organ with tilting tablets on quadrant jambs with adjustable stop-moving combination pistons operated on the "capture" system, but so far as I could gather, there is no specific Italian standard console.

In Switzerland I found mostly the German form, and in Belgium a combination of the French and German consoles. In Scandinavia, including Norway, Sweden and Denmark, a great variety of organ consoles exists. The organs of German manufacture, of which there are several very large examples, naturally have their own type of console with tilting tablet control.

Some Scandinavian builders also favour this form. Others prefer the French type of console with terraced stop-knobs, whilst consoles comprising a compound of both German and French control can also be found. In Denmark particularly the organ builders have reproduced some beautiful examples of the classical organ of the so-called Baroque period. Many of these have stop-knobs on straight jambs, similar in many respects to those built in England during the latter part of the eighteenth century. Unfortunately I have visited neither Russia nor Spain, but so far as I can find out by reading and correspondence, some form of the German type of organ seems to predominate in these countries. Naturally I found this to be so in Austria.

Both the tonal and mechanical features of their organs have unquestionably influenced Continental composers, and it is hoped that this chapter will in some measure help the student to acquire a grasp of the composers' intentions, for, as I have said before, "It is the music," (rather than the medium) "that matters."

CHAPTER XX

THE BAROQUE REVIVAL

D URING the last two decades a good deal of attention has been given to the study of the pipework of organs built during the so-called baroque period, and particularly to the work of Schnitger and the Silbermanns in Germany. Such instruments were of necessity voiced on light wind pressure, and the pipes were constructed accordingly. The chief characteristic was a beautifully clear, singing quality of tone. Colour was obtained by abundant mutation ranks, and silvery mixtures. The reeds were generally of very thin tone. When in tune the ensemble was quite remarkable, and produced a rich ringing effect of great brilliance without any scream, which gave an impression of being more powerful than was actually the case. The clarity of this ensemble made it especially suitable for polyphonic music. This led the German organ builders, notably Walcker, Steinmeyer, Kemper, Klais and others to make remarkably faithful reproductions of this fine old work. They even made exact copies of small Portativ and Positiv instruments, and incorporated baroque divisions and Rück Positiv manuals into some of their larger instruments with great success. I remember about 1938 playing a fine example in Berlin, where a very large and complete modern two-manual and pedal organ stood in a gallery opposite to a replica of a two-manual and pedal baroque organ. Both were played from a four-manual console, the upper keyboards being used for the baroque example, and the two lower for the modern organ. The pedal clavier, of course, controlled both baroque and ordinary pedal stops. The result was highly satisfactory.

Led mainly by Senator Emerson L. Richards, Donald

Harrison of the Aeolian Skinner Co., and Holtkamp, considerable advance has been made along these lines in America. Much greater attention has been given to a clarified ensemble, and quasi-baroque Positiv and Rück Positiv divisions have been added to existing organs, as well as being incorporated into the schemes of new instruments. Also as in Germany complete small baroque organs have been reproduced.

Not very much has been done in England. There are, however, one or two such examples, such as Lady Susi Jeans's baroque organ at Dorking, Surrey.

For many years there was a strong and utterly false idea prevalent among organ builders that low wind pressures and electric action were incompatible. That this is entirely erroneous was amply demonstrated by the writer in a lecture model, made to his design well over twenty years ago by T. C. Wilcock of Sheffield, and since destroyed by enemy action.

Most of our greater builders however have included separate mutation ranks in the choir organs of their larger schemes during the last two decades. A considerable increase in the number of mutation ranks, and a further development of compound stops, is anticipated by the Compton Organ Co. in the future.

Many players (and some builders) fondly imagine that, if a nazard $2\frac{2}{3}$ ft and a tierce $1\frac{3}{5}$ ft are made available on the choir organ, they will produce the effect of a baroque organ, but this is not so. Although these harmonics form part of the baroque tonal structure, unless they and the stops with which they have to combine are made, voiced, and finished on baroque lines, the resultant effect will not be baroque, however pleasing it may be.

The organ designer has to be on his guard against fads. There are unfortunately some who would actually alter the design of the noble organs of English or American artistic builders, in order to convert them into quasi-baroque instruments. That this has in fact been done is a tragedy. The baroque revival should be considered, not as an end in itself, but as a valuable means of adding variety to the scheme of the modern organ, by thus including bright, scintillating, and telling effects. The best work of our greatest builders has evolved a noble artistic tradition, well worthy of preservation, and should be treated with respect. To this artistic work baroque sections or divisions may well be added without in any way disfiguring the work of great craftsmen; and in the planning and designing of new organs, clarity of ensemble should undoubtedly be a guiding principle.

The following is a list of the more important baroque organ registers, as given in the writer's book *The Electric Organ* (3rd Edition) where also can be seen a sketch of the actual pipes forming these stops.

LIST OF BAROQUE STOPS

	ft		ft
Nachthorn	4, 2	Gemshorn	2
Schwiegel	2	†Flach Flute	2
Sifflöte	2	Dulcian Flute	8, 4
Nazard	2⅔	Spitz Quint	1⅓
Tierce	1⅗	†Gedacktpommer	4
*Quer Flute	2		
*Schweizerpfeife	1	REEDS	
Koppel Flute	2	Euphone	16, 8
Spillflöte	2	†Ranket	16, 8
†Quintade	16, 8, 4	Regal	8
Rohr Flute (Chimney Flute)	8, 4	Rohr Schalmey	8
Spitz Flute	8, 4	* Overblowing to Octaves	
Block Flute	4, 2	† Also on Pedal	

In addition to the above, several varieties of baroque mixture stops are made with three or more ranks.

The flue stops chiefly consist of a number of flute-toned

registers differently voiced so as to bring into prominence certain harmonics, together with fluty diapasons. Some of the flutes are stopped or half-stopped. They combine extremely well, and afford a number of clear, almost bell-like ensembles. These are most valuable in the performance of early polyphonic music. They are also useful in many compositions of Bach and his contemporaries.

The tone of the old reeds is somewhat uneven, very thin, and rich in harmonics, though when in tune it blends well with the flue-work. Personally, I found the modern examples far superior to any of the true period baroque reeds I have so far tried or heard.

What has been written about the use of mutation registers in Chapter VIII, applies *a fortiori* to baroque stops proper. No useful purpose would be served by suggesting a number of suitable combinations here. Trial and experiment with the stops themselves is the only safe guide, always bearing in mind the actual music these registers have to adorn.

The stops of the baroque section may sometimes be coupled to appropriate registers drawn on other departments of the organ, either to give piquancy, or to enhance the general beauty of the effect. This applies not only to the use of single stops, but also to a variety of bigger combinations and even to the baroque *tout ensemble*.

In attempting to imitate baroque effects on an ordinary English organ, the player can only experiment with the actual stops of the particular organ he is called upon to play.

The trial of any $2\frac{2}{3}$, 2, or $1\frac{3}{5}$ ft stops, combined with flute stops of 8 and 4, or even 16 ft pitch, will often afford reasonably good results, and these combinations should be fully tested. Above all, the enclosed mixture similarly combined should be so tried out, nor should the modification of the power of these stops by the appropriate balanced swell pedal be overlooked. The high-pitched stops so modified may well be coupled to suitable flutes or very quiet diapasons on an open soundboard (say great or choir).

Certain vox humana stops (when in perfect tune) will approximate the tone of baroque reeds, if used without tremulant, and can sometimes be added to the above synthetic baroque effects. Though the word Baroque has no actual significance in organ terminology, and is (as stated above) generally associated in England with the work of the Silbermann and Schnitger families, one important fact is often overlooked by writers and enthusiasts alike. This is that the organ building of this same period in Germany, France, Holland, Scandinavia, and so on, afforded differences in tonal characteristics much in the same manner (within limits) as to-day we have the English, French, German, or American schools of organ building.

Since the second great war the Scandinavian builders, notably Messrs. Marcussen, and Th. Frobenius and Co., have reproduced some strikingly successful examples of the classical ensemble of the baroque period. They have also realized the importance of placing the several departments of the organ in their true classical positions. The Rück Positiv for instance, can never give its true effect unless placed forward into the church or auditorium. Similarly, the Brustwerk, if not situated in the breast of the organ, can be no real Brustwerk. Messrs. Frobenius have built a number of charming instruments where this desideratum has been fully realized. Again, the Scandinavian reproductions of baroque reeds (like the German) possess a beauty and stability I have rarely found in true period reeds.

CHAPTER XXI

IN CONCLUSION

ANYONE who has read this book will, I hope, have glimpsed something of the wonder of the amazing instrument we call the organ. He will also have realized something of the variety of effects which can be obtained, even on an instrument of modest dimensions. If it has encouraged him to investigate the possibilities of registration in his own organ (be it large or small) and to exploit these to the full in real music, my object will have been largely attained. Once again it is the music and its interpretation that matters most.

The purely artistic point of view is, of course, of the utmost importance. It must, however, always be borne in mind that the music is being rendered on an instrument hallowed by long service in assisting man in his approach to, and in his worship of Almighty God. The organ itself may indeed be regarded as dedicated to that high purpose. Despite the lack of appreciation, and also the lack of adequate remuneration generally tendered to the church organist, we cannot offer to the Almighty anything less than our best. This means hard work and careful thought. It is important, not only thoroughly to master the technique of manuals and pedal, but that of registration also. Lemare insisted on the essential need of practising stop-changing assiduously, to avoid breaking the rhythm of the music, just as Best in his day had given practical proof of how it could be done.

The uninteresting and slipshod way in which too many organists are content to accompany psalms and hymns, shows the great need for the study of effective registration, quite apart from recital work. Players are apt to rely too exclusively on what is given by a very few fixed combination devices, and even then, the changes are often made at inappropriate places, and sometimes carelessly, even on the last chord of a phrase, instead of the first chord of the next! It cannot be too strongly emphasized that, to get the best out of any organ, the player will of necessity have recourse to much *hand* registration—pistons, etc., however numerous, will not do it all. Fortunately, there are some players who realize this to the full. Even in the simplest hymns they endeavour by original and subtle registration to make the sacred words they are accompanying reach the hearts of singers and listeners alike. They are indeed the "great" among us. Truly, such effort is worth while, for the end is, or should be—"*ad majorem Dei gloriam*—To the greater glory of God."

INDEX

Abbott and Smith, 43
Action, 4
  electro-pneumatic, 4, 7, 9
  mechanical, 4
  tubular-pneumatic, 4, 7
Adjustable combinations, 70, 71
Albert Hall—
  Royal, London, 40, 43, 52
  Sheffield, 49
Alexandra Palace, London, 40
American organs, 90
Atlantic City (World's largest organ),
    Frontispiece
Auslöser, 102

Bach, *Choral Preludes*, 56, 58
Bairstow, Sir Edward, 55, 61
Barker, J. S., 7
Baroque, 108
  reeds, 68, 111, 112
  stops (List of), 110
Belgian organs, 106
Birmingham Town Hall organ, 81
Bishop, 69
Blind combinations, 105
Bombard organ, 61
Boot, reed, 13
Bournemouth Pavilion, 14
Bridge, Sir Frederick, 91
Brindley and Foster, 16, 106

Cambridge, King's College, 81
Cancels, 75, 76
Capture system (combination), 70,
    71
Cavaillé-Coll, 7, 12, 49, 67
Chimes, 90
Chorus reeds, 36
Clarinet, 13, 43
Cocker, Norman, 35
Combination couplers, 74
Composition pedals, 69
Compton, 14, 19, 40, 56, 74, 76, 77,
    80, 109

Conacher, 17
Conclusion, 113
Continental ensembles, 37
Continental stop control, 93–107
Cor anglais, 43
Coupled system, 12, 13, 14
Couplers, 3, 59, 60
Crescendo pedal, 78
Crescendo roller, 102
Cymbale, 52
Cymbalstern, 92

Diapasons, 3, 10, 34, 35
Diaphones, 10, 13, 14
Direct electric action, 10
Dixon, Lieut.-Col. George, vii
Doncaster Parish Church, 52, 55,
    Plate III
Doubles "off," 78
Double touch, 80–6
Drawstop action, 6, 11
Dupré, Marcel, 88
Durham Cathedral, 40

Echo organ, 61, 66
Edinburgh, M'Ewan Hall, 14
Electro-pneumatic action, 4, 7, 9
Ellingford, H. F., 87
Ely Cathedral, 40, 52
Ensembles, continental, 37
Evans and Barr, 36
Extensions, pedal, 55

Floating divisions, 61
Flue pipes, 11
Flute, 3, 35
Flute-toned stops, 43–5
Freie Kombinationen, 103
French console, Plate VI
French horn, 43
French organ, 93–5
French stop control, 95–100
Frobenius, 112
Full great, 69

Full organ, 3, 37, 39, 64
Full swell, 36, 69

GAMBA, 3
General crescendo pedal, 78
General pistons, 73, 74
German organs, 101
German stop control, 102–4
Gongs, 90
Grace, Dr. Harvey, 39

HAMILTON, David, 7
Harp, 90
Harrison, Arthur, 40
Harrison, Donald, 108
Harrison and Harrison, 66, 72, 75, 81
Heavy pressure reeds, 28, 29
Hele, 17
Hereford Cathedral, 71
Holland, 106
Hollins, Alfred, 79
Hope-Jones, 10, 14, 16, 17, 20, 40,
    56, 80

KEY, 4
    chest, 8
    pallet, 8
King's College, Cambridge, 81

LEEDS, Parish Church, 61
Lemare, Edwin H., 67
Lincoln Cathedral, 75
Liverpool—
    Cathedral, 40, Plate I
    St. George's Hall, 87
Luminous stop control, 18, 19, 20

MAGNET, 9
Manchester Cathedral, 102
Marcussen, 112
Mechanical action, 4
Mixtures, 3, 51
Motors, pneumatic, 8
Mutation stops, 47–50

NORWICH Cathedral, 90, 102

OBOE, 13
Octave and sub octave couplers, 59,
    60, 62, 63, 64
Orchestral oboe, 13, 43

PALLET, 6
Parratt, Sir Walter, 33
Passau Cathedral, Plate VII
Pedal—
    couplers, 60, 77
    extensions, 55
    mixtures, 56
    mutations, 56
    quint, 56
    reeds, 57
    sostenuto, 87
    stops, 32, 54, 57
Percussions, 90–2
Pipes, 4, 10
Pipe scales, 12
Pneumatic lever, 7
Pyne, Dr. Kendrick, 33

QUINTATON, 45

REEDS, 12, 13
    imitative, 43
    pedal, 57, 58
Register, 3
Reversible pistons, 76, 77
Richards, Emerson L., 108
Roller crescendo, 102
Rothwell, 17
Rushworth and Dreaper, 76
Rutt, R. Spurden, 20

ST. BEES, Priory, 72, 75, 77
St. George's Hall, Liverpool, 87
St. John's, Birkenhead, 16
St. Lawrence, Nuremberg, 53
St. Martin-in-the-Fields, London,
    Plate V
St. Nicholas, Whitehaven, 75
St. Paul's Cathedral, London, 38
Scandinavian organs, 106
Schnitger, 108, 112
Schulze, 52, 55
Second touch, 80–6
Silbermann, 108, 112
Skinner, Ernest M., 43, 88
Sliders, 6–7
Southampton, Guildhall, 14, Plate II
Steinmeyer, 108
Sticker, 6

Stop, 3
  control,
    continental, 93–107
    French, 95–100
    German, 102–6
  keys, 16
Stops, list of, 22–30
String mixture, 52
String-tone stops, 21, 40–2
Sustainers, 87–9
Swiss organs, 106
Sydney (N.S.W.), Town Hall organ,
  Plate VIII

TILTING tablets, 17
Tracker action, 4
Tremulant, 3, 43, 66–7
Trompette militaire, 43 (footnote)
Trumpet, 3, 13
Truro Cathedral, 7
Tuba, 13, 38, 39
Tubular pneumatic action, 4, 7

VENTILS (French), 95
Violes, 10
Voix célestes, 41
Vox humana, 41, 67, 112

WALCKER, 108
Walker, J. W., 17, 76
Walze, 102
Westminster Abbey, 61, 90, 91
Wilcock, T. C., 109
Willis, 17, 40, 66, 71, 75, 81
Willis, Vincent, 7
Windchests, 4
Wind supply, 4
Windsor Castle, St. George's Chapel
  Plate IV

YORK Minster, 3, 55, 66

ZÜGE, 105